SUSTENANCE AND HOPE
FOR CAREGIVERS
OF ELDERLY PARENTS

For Jesse & Henry

Warmest wishes

Heres to our life

Gloria
6/30/09

Recent Titles in
The Praeger Series on Contemporary Health and Living

Polio Voices: An Oral History from the American Polio Epidemics
and Worldwide Eradication Efforts
Julie Silver, MD, and Daniel Wilson, PhD

Jihad and American Medicine: Thinking Like a Terrorist to Anticipate Attacks via
Our Health System
Adam Frederic Dorin, MD

Understanding the Antioxidant Controversy: Scrutinizing the "Fountain of Youth"
Paul E. Milbury and Alice C. Richer

The Criminalization of Medicine: America's War on Doctors
Ronald T. Libby

When the Diagnosis Is Multiple Sclerosis: Help, Hope, and Insights from
an Affected Physician
Kym E. Orsetti Furney, MD

Understanding Fitness: How Exercise Fuels Health and Fights Disease
Julie Silver, MD and Christopher Morin

A Guide to Weight Loss Surgery: Professional and Personal Views
Rhonda L. Hamilton, MD, MPH

An Introduction to Botanical Medicines: History, Science, Uses, and Dangers
Antoine Al-Ache

Understanding the Cesarean Section Controversy: Making Informed Decisions
Nicette Jukelevics

Understanding the High-Functioning Alcoholic
Sarah Allen Benton

The Pain Detective; Every Ache Tells a Story: Understanding How Stress
and Emotional Hurt Become Chronic Physical Pain
Hillel M. Finestone, MDS

SUSTENANCE AND HOPE FOR CAREGIVERS OF ELDERLY PARENTS

The Bread of Angels

GLORIA G. BARSAMIAN

The Praeger Series on Contemporary Health and Living
Julie Silver, MD, Series Editor

PRAEGER
An Imprint of ABC-CLIO, LLC

A B C C L I O

Santa Barbara, California • Denver, Colorado • Oxford, England

Library of Congress Cataloging-in-Publication Data

Barsamian, Gloria G.
  Sustenance and hope for caregivers of elderly parents : the bread of angels
      p. cm. — (The Praeger series on contemporary health and living)
  Includes bibliographical references and index.
  ISBN 978-0-313-36011-4 (alk. paper) — ISBN 978-0-313-36012-1 (ebook)
  1. Aging parents—Care.   2. Adult children of aging parents—Family relationships.
3. Caregivers—Psychology.   4. Aging parents—Psychology.   5. Caregivers—Family
relationships.   6. Aging parents—Family relationships.   I. Title.
  HQ1063.6.B37   2009
  649.8084'6—dc22   2009012265

13 12 11 10 09   1 2 3 4 5

This book is also available on the World Wide Web as an eBook.
Visit www.abc-clio.com for details.

ABC-CLIO, LLC
130 Cremona Drive, P.O. Box 1911
Santa Barbara, California 93116-1911

This book is printed on acid-free paper ∞
Manufactured in the United States of America

You other few who turned your minds in time unto the *bread of angels*, which provides men here with life—but hungering for more—you may indeed commit your vessel to the deep salt-sea, keeping your course within my wake, ahead of waves smooth again.

—Dante Alighieri, *Paradiso*

CONTENTS

Series Foreword

Over the past 100 years, there have been incredible medical breakthroughs that have prevented or cured illness in billions of people and helped many more improve their health while living with chronic conditions. A few of the most important 20th-century discoveries include antibiotics, organ transplants, and vaccines. The 21st century has already heralded important new treatments including such things as a vaccine to prevent human papillomavirus from infecting and potentially leading to cervical cancer in women. Polio is on the verge of being eradicated worldwide, making it only the second infectious disease behind smallpox to ever be erased as a human health threat.

In this series, experts from many disciplines share with readers important and updated medical knowledge. All aspects of health are considered, including subjects that are disease-specific and preventive medical care. Disseminating this information will help individuals to improve their health as well as researchers to determine where there are gaps in our current knowledge and policy makers to assess the most pressing needs in health care.

Series Editor Julie K. Silver, MD
Assistant Professor,
Harvard Medical School
Department of Physical Medicine and Rehabilitation

ACKNOWLEDGMENTS

I want to thank my acquisitions editor, Debbie Carvalko at ABC-CLIO, who was the force behind this book. She believed and had faith in me and gave me sustenance during a whole year of writing and rewriting. My thanks to Julie Silver, MD for giving me this opportunity. *Sustenance and Hope for Caregivers of Elderly Parents* is better than it might have been because of Peter Zheutlin, who was always right with infuriating regularity. He read the drafts and gave precise and insightful comments.

I owe the biggest debt of gratitude to the thousands of extraordinary men and women who let me into their personal lives. Their stories filled my heart. They taught me that we cannot afford to play the old games of ageism any longer. Instead of flourishing in old age, holding onto youth and refusing to admit or acknowledge that aging is a valid process can only lead to desperation. Though aging is biological, it is not a time bomb. It has become a social phenomenon. We have become afraid to grow old. It was not death that people in my studies feared, but "who would take care of them" when they grew old. This is a self-fulfilling prophecy. Instead, as we grow older, through our own actions, we can create a new image as we move into the future; the future that we helped to create. Without dreading the future, and by using the wisdom accumulated by many years of experience to change patterns of conversation, change outdated rules, and bring into existence new adventures for ourselves, we can debunk ageism for ourselves and those coming after us. As we do this, we will find that we will not be stuck in the past. We move into a future, not as martyrs putting up with old ways, but as collaborators, mutually giving sustenance to each other. If what was thought to be irreversible deterioration in people in nursing homes could be reversed by just giving a plant to care for, as Ellen Langer has shown, imagine what the new paradigm for aging could be. Future generations depend on us to find those clues for a new paradigm of aging not only for their survival but for the survival of the species.

The Lahey Clinic Center backed me up in every new start-up program I initiated at the hospital, and for 28 years I had the pleasure and benefit of being part of an intimate community of dedicated professionals; though there were too many to mention here, they included Dr. John Libertino, Dr. David Steinberg, Dr. John Przbylski, Dr. Robert Wise, Dr. Robert Schreiber, Ann Marie Brady, Penny Abrams, Pamela Resnick, Benjamin Foster, and Abby Rodman.

Sabrena Johnson prepared and read the final manuscript. She is a calming and efficient and a thorough assistant. She kept my spirits up and read and typed every draft. Special thanks to Carly Goteiner and Elisa Kreisinger, who early on typed the first drafts and helped me become computer-savvy. They were experts on tracking down research and information on the Internet. Thanks to the staff at Apex CoVantage for their production work on my book, particularly the project manager, Mary Cotofan, and the editorial coordinator, Amanda Foxcroft. Copyeditor Stephanie Ernst completed the editing professionally and skillfully. A special thanks to Ann Noder for her stellar performance in taking the book forward. I am grateful for all the help afforded me by the one-to-one assistants at the Apple Stores in Florida and Massachusetts. Ashod Balanian kept my computer tuned and always showed up in a crisis.

I am very grateful to Rose Romano and Barbara Kassler, who are my friends both old and new.

Without Barbara, I would be very lonely and isolated in a new community, and she held me up in so many ways almost every day I wrote. Her wisdom and support made me stronger. Rose, my oldest and dearest friend, inspired me with her daily upbeat e-mails that filled me with laughter. Her friendship, support, wisdom, and humor are part of this book. I hope I can grow older and wiser with them. Cleo Cabile took care of my household and kept things running smoothly. Stanley Szymkowicz provided friendship in a quiet refined manner, and stood by my husband Bob through thick and thin. Regardless of Bob's disabilities, he was his best friend and constant companion during years of research and writing. I am deeply indebted to him. My friend Dr. David Gao opened doors for me while doing fieldwork on the elderly in China, Tibet, and Mongolia. I had the privilege of spending time with a barefoot doctor making calls on old people in rural China and visiting China's nursing homes, called "Happy Homes." The opportunity to study Confucianism with a Chinese sage and to visit a secret shrine that held 10-foot tablets of Confucius scriptures that were buried during the Chinese Revolution were some of the highlights of my life.

To protect the anonymity of the many people in my research, I have changed the names, and sometimes I made changes in the information. Where permission was needed, it was granted.

On a philosophical plane, I owe Gregory Bateson, Arthur Kleinman, Robert Butler, Deborah Tennen, Harriet Goldhor Lerner, and Ellen J. Langer, whose works and writings contributed to my thinking, and I hope this book provides the impetus for those who read it to continue to push forward in creating the changes that are on the horizon.

My devoted husband Bob, a faithful friend, was protective, humorous, and filled with his own wisdom and experience. He cooked for me a whole year while I was writing *Sustenance and Hope for Caregivers of Elderly Parents*. He stood by me with reassurance and faith even when I had very little in myself. We both grew through the process while ourselves growing older. Betty, Bob's sister, and her husband Steve provided good models of parenthood and growing old.

My children, Lisa, Stuart, Robert, and Joan, provided the most important things: love, loyalty, and warmth through my whole life. Stuart cheered me on every day with notes and sound computer advice. My siblings Lucille, Joanne, Pat, and Anthony and their families helped me stay focused on what really mattered in life. Joanne's daily early morning calls kept me on course.

I have been unduly fortunate to have the wise counsel of Lorraine Heilbrunn, who kept me safe while I crossed many narrow bridges in this world. Through her I learned that the most important thing was not to be afraid.

Introduction: Caregiving—A Major Social Issue

It is no longer uncommon for four generations of a family to be alive at the same time. The population of 65-year-olds and over is expected to double in size within the next 25 years in the United States, and the age group 85 and older is now the fastest growing segment of the U.S. population. As the baby boomers approach old age, they are facing one of the most complicated and multifaceted issues they have faced in their lives: caregiving and care-receiving.

Increasing longevity raises the prospect that two generations within a single family may need caregiving, placing increasing and potentially impossible burdens on those who may find themselves caring for both parents and grandparents. As more and more of us find ourselves in the role of caregiver or care receiver, we need to take a fresh look at the challenges inherent in such relationships, but we also need a new vision of caregiving: one that emphasizes the potential rewards, emotional and spiritual, that can accompany this most demanding of life's challenges.

A New Paradigm of Caregiving

Caretaking is fraught with many myths, assumptions, and beliefs that have prevented generations of caregivers from understanding that caregiving is a rite of passage. Rites of passage define a sense of self in relation to society, paving the way for life transitions and allowing a more meaningful and clear incorporation of both familial and public roles. Seeing a family member through a health crisis marks the beginning of yet another transition for both the caretaker and the receiver and helps to define new roles and responsibilities in each of their lives. Although caretaking can help younger caregivers understand their place in the world, most view it with dread: an emotional roller coaster in which a plethora of daunting practical issues must also be addressed. These issues include the needs of spouses and children, estate and legal matters, health insurance, medications, funeral arrangements, and, in many cases, conflicts with siblings about how best to care for Mom or Dad and how to apportion responsibility, financial and personal, for their care. Though caregiving is always a multifaceted challenge, it can also offer profound emotional and psychological rewards, and with the right perspective, it need not be confronted with unalloyed dread and anxiety. The key lies in going beyond these anxieties related to caregiving and developing supports that are relevant to our growing population in need of care.

Millions of Americans will end up in a caregiving or care-receiving situation eventually. Apprehension is understandable. How will we balance our own families, careers, and retirement dreams with the demands of caregiving? How will it interrupt our lives or defer our dreams? How will the emotional toll affect our families and ourselves? Will we have the emotional strength to provide care if a parent is debilitated for a long time? These are some of the natural questions that almost all of us ask ourselves. Typically, however, families do not address these complex issues until the crisis is upon them. Thus, one of the chief recommendations of this book is that families, if at all possible, begin the caregiving discussion well before a parent becomes ill. The typical caregiving situation is an adult child caring for an elderly parent, yet there are many permutations. For example, a parent might find him- or herself caring for both an adult child and that adult child's family; a spouse can be caring for his or her mate; or a grandchild may be caring for a grandparent. Regardless of the exact caregiving situation, this kind of early discussion can be very helpful.

As we age, it is natural to worry about what could happen to us and who will take care of us in our old age should we need help. But keeping these worries to ourselves does nothing to prepare our families for the caregiving challenges that may lie ahead. It can be enormously reassuring for all to give voice to these worries and to begin to plan for the future. As life circumstances change, the discussion can be renewed as often as necessary, so that as the future unfolds, all concerned feel confident that everyone's fears, expectations, and concerns have been aired.

Many families find that opening the conversation about caregiving requires a shift from long-established family dynamics that have prevented the family members from relating to each other. But once the conversation is in the open, the relationship between family members can be enriched and deepened. For caregivers and receivers, once new dynamics are established, the process becomes something to no longer fear. If a discussion starts early enough with the purpose of creating reciprocal advantages for both generations, caregiving can become a long-awaited and well-prepared source of renewal and meaning for both the caregiver and the care-receiver.

Along with opening a discussion, the social expectation that we should respond to one another in kind is the foundation of the new caregiving paradigm that is based on a mutual exchange of recognition and understanding. The care-receiver gives up his or her independence until the crisis has passed, and the caregiver understands the paradoxes and the helplessness that occurs with an illness. This reciprocity can heal broken relationships because in our culture, there is no common ritual for caretaking, and reciprocity can clear the way to promote a new kind of relationship between the generations. This reciprocity in caregiving emanates from a sense of shared responsibility, mutuality, and intimacy, not from a guilty conscience or role-reversal strategy where parents become like children.

In modern caregiving, there is rarely an open conversation prior to illness, and this concept of reciprocity is often lost among the emotions and stresses of caretaking. As people struggle to come to terms with the failing health of their loved ones, the new paradigm (opening a discussion, together with the concept of reciprocity) provides a societal mirror in which the adult child is reflected in the aging parent, and the aging parent is reflected in the adult child. Two people bonded in a caregiving situation have much to share with one another and thus may see themselves reflected in some way in the other. The caregivers may see their own future, and the care-receivers may see a younger version of themselves. Within the new paradigm, the dynamics within a family have an opportunity to shift and strengthen.

REINVENTING AND REDEFINING CAREGIVING

Throughout my 28-year career as a social worker at the Lahey Clinic in Burlington, Massachusetts, I saw more and more people caught ill prepared and ill equipped, physically and psychologically, to care for an elderly parent. Why were people so discouraged and overwhelmed? What were their fears? What were the fears of their parents? Why did so many reach the crisis point having given little thought to the caregiving challenge? Why did some families show compassion and concern, while other families remained indifferent? Why did some loving caregivers feel they were never doing enough? Why were they so drained and exhausted? Why did they feel so isolated? I addressed these questions during my practice and research at the Lahey Clinic and then, 20 years later, confronted those same questions as I cared for my own aging parents and husband.

Caregiving is changing, and this book will hopefully provide guidance to a new generation of caregivers as they assume one of the greatest challenges of their lives. By reevaluating the assumptions, myths, crises, and consequences of modern-day caregiving, a new generation can redefine caregiving and transform it from an experience approached with anxiety and dread to one of opportunity and reward.

1

REINVENTING AND REDISCOVERING THE CAREGIVING RELATIONSHIP

The fastest growing segment of the U.S. population is the age group 85 and older. Robert Butler, a Pulitzer Prize–winning author and president of the National Institute of Aging (NIA), calls this new phenomenon the Longevity Revolution. The NIA (2006) reports that by 2030, almost one out of every five Americans—some 72 million people—will be 65 or older. Today's baby boomers are healthier and living a more active and independent lifestyle, especially in comparison with their parents, who, like the other 14 million older Americans, have a high percentage of disability (NIA 2008). Because people are living longer, 50 million people are finding themselves caring for another family member, relative, or friend during any given year (NFCA 2001). These informal caregivers, who spend over $354 billion out of their own pockets, also make major changes in their work schedule, such as arriving late and leaving early, switching from full-time to part-time hours, turning down promotions, and choosing early retirement (NAC and AARP 2004). They spend an average of 1,080 hours per year on care (Gibson and Houser 2007). The National Family Caregivers Association (NFCA) states that 44 percent of men take on this role as caregiver. But this does not mean that women's roles in caregiving have decreased. Instead, the NFCA found that women spend 17 years caring for children and then an additional 18 helping an elderly parent (MetLife Juggling Act Study 1999). Caregiving and receiving is a major social issue affecting millions. We are approaching uncharted territory as our nation's population reaches old age and as their caregiving needs increase dramatically.

The good news is that contrary to popular belief, the caretaking relationship has potential benefits for both parties if the paradigm shifts. Reinventing and rediscovering caretaking means establishing an open conversation early on, before an illness strikes. Caring for an elderly parent or loved one magnifies the relationship between the generations whether it is positive or negative because the role of dependency is reversed. There is an emotional and physical strain on both parties because of this dependency, but with some preparation, caring for an elderly loved one can be a rewarding and life-altering experience for everyone involved.

Though caregiving relationships are on the rise, few are prepared for the role of caregiver. This lack of preparation exacerbates caregiver burnout, irritability, mood swings, sleep disturbances, depression, fatigue, and sexual dysfunction. Lack of preparation also intensifies existing family dynamics, sometimes for the better, but often for the worse. But illness can be an opportunity to break dysfunctional family patterns where the relationship between members may be strained or altered by unhealed wounds.

Perhaps the most important step any family can take to prepare for caregiving is to open the discussion before it becomes a reality. Talking to parents early about their wishes in the event of a debilitating illness, infirmity, or death eases anxiety. Conversations about helping with daily activities such as shopping, meal preparation, and medical appointments can reduce role ambiguity when multiple family members will eventually share caregiving responsibilities. As the caregiving situation changes over time, the need for dialogue continues. Some people can move past the early stages of caregiving, and some may settle in for the long haul.

Many times, the need for placement in a nursing home arises because of increased stress placed on the caregiver as a result of the many complex roles of caretaking. The tipping point comes when the caregiver burns out or when the care receiver needs around-the-clock care. When a patient becomes incontinent or cannot walk, feed, or bathe him- or herself, many caregivers have to rely on a nursing home because they can no longer continue providing hands-on care themselves. Often it is not their first choice, but it remains the only option for stressed-out caregivers and care-receivers too ill to remain at home.

However, no option should be permanent. Rehabilitation, even in a nursing home, offers the receivers time to regain strength and motivation in order to get back to their former way of life before their health declined. While the loved one is in rehab, the caregiver now has time to prepare psychologically and physically for the next phase of caregiving.

Discussing the challenges of caretaking roles can also be an opportunity to bring up issues regarding the importance of rehabilitation, finances, and legal documents. Often parents feel burdened by the responsibility of keeping things such as wills, funeral arrangements, and private possessions to themselves. Of the patients I interviewed, many found themselves talking about nothing in particular, but over time they were able share their care-receiving preferences. An adult daughter of an aging father who was critically ill told me she wished she could have been talking to her father "like this before he was ill." She reported that through these conversations, she gained information about the whereabouts of important legal documents and hidden assets that, in the end, helped her father continue to live in his own home with nursing care and paid caregivers.

However, if a childhood wound goes too deep or if adult children and aging parents are unable to communicate verbally without stormy and irrational behavior, for a caregiver to provide primary care to a loved one may not be the best solution. Instead, a contract similar to a prenuptial agreement can be instituted with the help of a lawyer in order to sort out care-receiving preferences as well as asset distribution. Although it may sound harsh and calculated, such a contract has worked as a last resort in some families who could not communicate.

Once the care arrangements were made, I found that there was a sense of hopelessness and helplessness in those adult children whose parents were discharged from the hospital. The study included those who went to a nursing home, a chronic care hospital, and/or a rehabilitation hospital and those parents who received services from the Visiting Nurse Association in their own homes. Many adult children reported that they became increasingly frustrated in dealing with the environment, the institutions, and the caretakers while negotiating for their ill parent. The dependency of an ill parent often disrupted the lives of all family members and became a threat to the integrity and functionality of the family system. This in turn produced changes in the families' accustomed structure, patterns, and roles. Adult children had many concerns and complained that they could not balance everything in their lives even though their parents were being cared for in a facility. Seventy-six percent of these adult children found themselves assuming the role of parent, exhibiting role reversal (Barsamian 1985). A high percentage of these adult children reported that not only the ill parent, but also other members in the family, required more emotional support. There was also a measurement of pessimism regarding the adult children's future. Many adult children said that they could not imagine what life would be like for them in 10 years. Both men and women who had assumed the role of caretaker in the middle of their lives found the task of caretaking demanding, and they reported experiences of burnout, helplessness, and depression. The following quotation is from a son who is representative of what most people said:

> During my father's lengthy illness and hospital stay, I found myself feeling more lonely and isolated than I had ever felt before. When it was discovered that my father had cancer and that it was probably terminal, I expected family and friends would rally to our support. Instead, I found the opposite to be true. A few people were supportive but most wanted as little as possible to do with me and my father. Even though I can understand their reasons and recognize that people were uncomfortable with illness and death, my resentment was deep. I'm sure that my experience was not uncommon and it would have been helpful to talk to others who had faced a similar situation.

Adult children in my study felt unprepared and, thus, incompetent (Barsamian & Kelly 1988). They agreed that talking with their parent about financial and caregiving options long before the medical crisis could have reduced this sense of hopelessness, helplessness, and incompetence. My findings have been confirmed by many investigators (see Neugarten 1979). The elderly parents, on the other hand, told me they did not want to be a burden to their children. I developed a short life-review document with most of the patients I met at the hospital. Through this review, I found that elderly parents felt extremely unhappy that their life no longer revolved around their previously established social network, where they were involved in their children's lives as well as the lives of their friends and family. Most aging parents felt knitted into the social structure through their relationships with their children, family, and acquaintances and through the roles they performed in these relationships. Many older persons tended to expect more from their children because of increased dependence resulting from illness. The sick spouses, on the other hand, shared that they did not want to be a burden to their partners.

For those families thinking about options for care upon discharge from a hospital, those who need long-term care usually have complex medical problems that cannot be treated at home. Good long-term care makes a difference in the lives of those who need it and impacts their families as well. The touchstone of long-term care is still a nursing home, but rehabilitation hospitals offer a short-term formal program that usually includes a very active program of rehabilitation including physical therapy, occupational therapy, and speech therapy. Many insurance plans will cover these expenses as long as the patient is able to endure at least three hours of active rehabilitation. It allows the patient to return home with more strength and the ability to be more active and therefore relieves some of the stress on the caregiver. The caregiver has time to prepare for the incoming patient while he or she is in the rehabilitation center.

Assisted living facilities offer services to a group of older people who are still autonomous. A good, modern, well-run facility can be a welcome haven for those who can no longer completely fend for themselves and/or are lonely. Unless one has insurance to cover the cost, which is expensive, one must pay privately. Many residents of assisted facilities are able to stay in their own surroundings even when they are in decline as long as they bring in personal care workers.

Sustaining a loved one at home, even with hired help, works best with a caregiver available. There are a lot of communication options for the caregiver to keep in contact with the patient. A good social system, including family, friends, neighbors, and volunteers, often plays an important role in allowing the patient to be at home as long as possible, in an environment that is comfortable and supportive to the patient's needs.

Because most people want to stay in their own homes as long as possible, a combination of home, family care, and private care may be an option. Caregiving takes a community, and no one, not even the care-receiver or caregiver, should be isolated. There should not be a tradeoff between quality of life and quality of care. Good care must be actively pursued.

Although the percentage of elderly parents living in the same household as their children has declined, the percentage of those living within a 10-minute driving radius has increased. Honoring patients' choices while monitoring their safety allows for both parties to feel liberated from the constraints and stresses of care. Providing long-distance care does not increase patients' probability of having an accident for they could just as well have an accident in a nursing home. Uprooting a parent from his or her own environment can be frightening for the parent. However, in many cases it is necessary to find a more suitable environment, such as a nursing center. Talking with patients about their preferences for care, the location of which can be in their own community or closer to their family's home, can help a loved one go through the transition.

Caregiving and care-receiving play vital roles in our lives, from the cradle to the grave. In sickness and anxiety, people often become demanding of others, and when the condition becomes a turning point where danger and death lurk, the elderly parent will almost certainly seek proximity to a trusted person— usually their adult children. The relationship between the caregiver and care-receiver brings us face to face with the reflections of ourselves and provides us with a greater reflection of society. Renegotiating these relations and redefining caregiving can eliminate the myths that keep us from truly tending to the elderly. In contrast, in China, filial responsibility toward one's parents while they are living include "(1) not only love but also reverence; (2) not only material support, but consolation; (3) the elimination of all bad habits so as not to affect one's parents as a result of ones own humiliation or injury; (4) care of one's own health, so as not to cause one's parents any anxiety; and (5) remonstrance to parents with gentleness if there is disagreement with them" (Li Fu Chen 396). Although families have their own histories that shape them, our society portrays the old, the ill, and the disabled as invisible and unproductive. These characterizations destroy human worth and create a society that is unprepared to care for them. By making the choice to reverse the current trends, we affirm that human value is not tied solely to self-efficacy and that human needs are not a burden.

2

ADULT CHILDREN
AND ELDERLY PARENTS

Illness is the nightside of life, a more onerous citizenship. Everyone who is born holds dual citizenship, in a kingdom of the well and in the kingdom of the sick.

—Susan Sontag, "Illness as a Metaphor"

The respectful do not despise others. The frugal do not plunder others. The prince who treats men with spite and plunders them is only afraid that they may not prove obedient to him—how can he be regarded as respectful or frugal? How can respectfulness and frugality be made out of tones of the voice and a smiling manner?

—Mencius, *The Book of Mencius*

Imagine you are in a hospital bed. The young intern is telling you and your children that for insurance reasons, you must leave the hospital you entered three days ago following a mild stroke. Although there was no permanent damage from the stroke, you are still unable to walk without assistance, and your speech is slurred. Your doctor recommends you enter a rehabilitation center and then receive additional assistance when you return home. Your children look upset, and your son asks the doctor if you could stay in the hospital for a few more days to build up your strength. The doctor explains that insurance regulations will not permit you to remain in the hospital unless you are still ill but offers the services of a social worker and nurse care manager who will help you in making a caretaking decision. The care manager offers your family a list of rehabilitation centers and informs you and your family that you must leave the hospital in the morning. You defer to your children to make the decision. You are telling them that whatever they decide will be fine when, suddenly, your daughter walks out. In the hallway, you overhear her say, "Shoot me first before I ever come to this!" The remaining family members and social worker in the room continue on uncomfortably.

This situation was a reality for the Chase family. As I helped the family make their decision, Virginia, the daughter who had walked out of the room, returned. The facility she chose along with her siblings was close to her home. After making the decision, she took me aside and apologized for her behavior, explaining she was frustrated and angry at the "circumstances." Virginia loved her mother but felt unprepared to take on the responsibility of caring for her. After raising her own children, it was the first time in Virginia's married life that she did not have family obligations. Her mother was always there for her, and she wanted to reciprocate, but "this timing was bad." She said she "would never send [her] mother to a nursing home," but the truth was that she could not take her mother into her home. "I feel incredibly guilty for this," Virginia said. The family had never discussed or prepared for the possibility that their mother might someday need caregiving. Having this discussion would have saved both Virginia and her mother much emotional stress.

Once her children left, Mary confided to me that she would "rather die" than be a burden to her family. She did not want her children to "give up their lives" to care for her. Although she shared these feelings with me, she had not shared them with her children. As I spoke with Mary in the empty room, tears rolled down her face. She had overheard her daughter's frustration and said she was "so sorry to be a burden to her family." As a parent she felt she "sacrificed everything" for her children. She had been a caretaker for her parents and then her husband, so she knew what a commitment caretaking was. When her husband died, she had felt a sense of power and freedom that she had never felt before. Now, in the hospital and dependent on her children, she felt like she had no choices. "I would prefer to die rather than upset or hurt my children," she said. As we talked about her options, she was very excited about making some of her own decisions. Her stroke provided the crisis she needed to start thinking about her own "old age." She did not want anyone to "give up their lives" for caregiving as she had done.

Virginia was still acting out previous feelings from her past as the oldest child and had a list of accumulated resentments from childhood that came up in her interviews; these are the same feelings and resentments that other adult children have expressed time and time again. One recurring complaint was that a parent would make an adult child feel trapped and controlled by using a past martyrdom against them, making them feel guilty no matter what the adult child did. Comments from the parent such as "you don't care for anyone but yourself" sting. The underlying message is "if you loved me, you would do what I say every single time." When caretakers internalize this guilt, they behave as a parent's rescuer and become on call 24 hours a day. The adult children become victims when daily complaints from the elderly parent consistently reinforce guilt. Although it is important to recognize that elderly parents will not change, especially when ill, refraining from reacting automatically will prevent caretakers from getting caught up in the melodrama of family affairs.

Many adult children and parents are as close as Mary and her family, but often too much closeness can feel like someone is trying to control you. In

Mary's case, what she heard from her children was "they want to put me in a nursing home." She retreated from her former self where she felt competent and important, and her frustration was so intense that she moved backward, relying on her children as she had done with her husband. Her daughter, without notice, was doing and saying things, such as storming out of the room, that were hurting Mary's feelings. Virginia was angry but was also busy with her own life. Virginia told me her response of walking out of the room and yelling had often worked for her as a child. "My parents would give me a great deal of attention, and I would eventually get my way," she told me. I have found that children's habits from childhood resurface in such situations and become a coping mechanism for adult children such as Virginia.

Virginia was able to recognize that her mother was not only a parent but also an aging woman, and since being widowed, Mary had changed and grown into a sage. Virginia and her mother were alike in many ways. As Mary's recovery progressed, she no longer needed round-the-clock care. She and Virginia decided to use some of the money that was saved to hire private help, so that Virginia could work, and her mother could stay in her own home. The tensions that had developed between the two generations earlier that year (after the stroke) were obvious and potentially harmful, especially to Mary. Eventually the tension relaxed, however, and when Virginia was able to sort out her past childhood emotions, it allowed space for a meaningful and reciprocal relationship to develop between the two generations.

In this reciprocal relationship between the generations, Virginia realized her mother had a new identity. Mary created a new image of aging by not being a victim of circumstance. While living in Virginia's home, Mary was able to forge open talks with her daughter. As a result of her strength in overcoming a stroke, she became a sage of her generation. Mary realized she was powerful in making decisions for herself. She was becoming accustomed to growth and change and thus resisted learned helplessness. Her wisdom, strength, spirituality, and flexibility replaced the old way of martyrdom, where guilt is often used against the caregiver. Mary's approach is one way to replace old ways of thinking about caregiving with new, healthier possibilities.

Caregiving and care-receiving are emotionally and spiritually rewarding experiences. To realize this, both parties have to be honest with their feelings and with one another. The care-receiver needs to be cognizant of the demands being placed on the caregiver. Caregivers should recognize that if they have negative attitudes, such attitudes will reinforce the helplessness of the sick person. If a person is feeling sorry for himself or herself, it reinforces the feelings of anger and resentment toward those who care for that person.

There are a multitude of families and patients who become so overwhelmed and anxious when a parent needs care that frustration, anger, resentment, and helplessness can often surface and find no resolution. Many of these feelings cause bitterness to resurface in other areas of the family's life. Caregivers need to talk with their loved ones and be realistic about the feelings they have but also about the feelings that the care-receiver has. Most elderly parents who need physical care also need emotional support from outside the caretaking re-lationship. Caregivers need support as well, given that they are twice as likely to suffer from depression, anxiety, or other health problems as a result of the strains of providing for both their own families and their parents.

A positive attitude and an honest relationship between the caregiver and receiver are beneficial for the physical and psychological health of both parties. Pessimism makes the caregiver sick and the care-receiver bitter, in-terfering with a family's coping skills and causing serious problems in other relationships. We all have emotional legacies from our families that color our expectations and perceptions.

When I met with Edward, who described his father as a womanizer who frequently abused his mother, he was very pessimistic about finding a solution for his father's future. Edward was his mother's confidant his whole life and could not acknowledge anything good about his father, who was now para-lyzed from a severe stroke. He told me, "I wish he was dead." There was no comforting him. His mother refused to come in for a meeting with me because evidently too much had happened in the family's past. Edward cut himself off emotionally from his father and was negative and bitter toward the end. In navigating his relationship with his parents, he never talked straight to his father and kept a pessimistic attitude throughout his whole life. His father was transferred to a veterans' hospital and died there. Edward refused any therapy, and he never got a grip on his problems, which he again encountered later in his life, and this affected his two marriages.

Parents as perceived by middle-aged offspring become almost peers, and as they grow older and approach death, adult children may idolize them—or, as in Edward's case, may continue to punish them for events in the past. I found that Edward was unable to gradually forgive his father for his shortcomings, even though he could no longer hope for him to change. His solution was to wish for his father's death. Although some adult children find when they grow older themselves that their parents have done their best, some are unable to forgive their parents' mistakes and limitations. The price we pay, however, by continuing a strained and unloving relationship with our parents, is too high. Caregivers may have to give up anger, resentment, and annoyances and release the desire to punish and blame others around them. This is for every-one's health and well-being. As Confucius once said, "In serving your father and mother, you may gently admonish them. But if you see they have no in-tention of listening to you, then be respectful as before and do not disobey. You might feel distressed but should never feel resentful" (Watson, *The Analects of Confucius,* 34).

But some parents may be just plain stubborn and will not follow a caregiver's advice. I found this to be the case in instances where there was regression in both the caretaker's life and the care-receiver's life. When a family member can no longer fill their previously established roles, there is a shift in the family dy-namic. In the following story, it took the Jackson family a few tries before they were able to adapt to their new roles as caregiver and care-receiver.

The Jacksons are an elderly couple who were very anxious to get their son "off their back." The son claimed that his parents were always fighting. "I offer to do the grocery shopping for them, and they refuse. Two days later, they call and have no food." The conflict between his mother and father seemed to be the food his father was purchasing. His mother constantly complained about her husband's food choices when she provided a list. The husband claimed his wife was "aggressive and didn't appreciate all his efforts." He brought her to appointments, did all the grocery shopping, and cleaned the house because Mrs. Jackson was always too sick to do her normal routine. The stress in the household greatly contributed to her diabetes, which caused her blood sugars to be inconsistent, and she often required more insulin. She never really addressed what her needs were with her husband but constantly complained to her son. She felt her husband "took over everything," so she substituted anger for criticism of her husband's good deeds.

The tipping point for this family came when Mrs. Jackson was in danger of dying from acidosis. This is not unusual for families with a diabetic member. The cycles of stress were routine for them, and they could not talk openly with their son. In order to solve both the physical and the mental health issues embedded in the family dynamic, the family was connected to a nutritionist and an endocrinologist. The couple made a decision to join a support group. Mrs. Jackson went out with her friends once a week for lunch and eventually joined a bridge club. Her husband and son met with a therapist until they sorted out their differences, and Mr. Jackson took Mrs. Jackson with him to the market so that she could choose her own food. Because of her confidence and improved health, her husband was not needed as often and had the free time to play golf once a week.

Accumulating evidence shows that social support can enhance one's immune system and fight off illness. As time went on, Mrs. Jackson became an expert on her diabetes, and her eyesight improved because she had her blood levels under control. Even her husband, who had turned into a form of moral support, benefited. Although the fighting and bickering never fully ended, the family members had now established their own lives separate from each other.

My interactions with other families in the hospital made me realize that resentment and hostility were not helpful for caregivers or families who were already overwhelmed with pessimism, distrust, and stress. For these families, it was not easy to be fully active in the caretaking process because there were some other previous issues getting in the way.

In a family of four daughters, one refused to help in the care of her elderly mother who was suffering from ovarian cancer. The three other sisters set up a time chart so that their mother would never be alone. They also arranged the mother's home to suit her needs by placing the hospital bed in the sunroom so that their mother could look out on her flower gardens. The three daughters never confronted their sister but instead remained angry and resentful that she refrained from her caretaking responsibilities. They never understood or asked about their sister's little-known fear of their mother's death. Their mother died unexpectedly two days after arriving home from an emergency hospital admission. The three sisters felt that their sibling had been selfish in refusing to disrupt her busy life to help with the caregiving responsibilities. They remained unwilling to talk to each other, and eventually the lone sister withdrew from the family and became isolated; her children grew up not appreciating their aunts and never knowing their many cousins.

Although some siblings compare their efforts to each other, some elderly parents I found compared themselves to their adult children. Mrs. Cameron was very unhappy that her daughter divorced her abusive husband. She had stayed in an abusive marriage for over 60 years and constantly compared herself to her adult daughters, which caused her children much bitterness and anguish. Elderly parents must accept the fact that they cannot have everything that their children might have.

However, some elderly people I worked with tried to set goals for themselves, such as witnessing a grandchild graduate college or a grandson get married, in an effort to extend their lives beyond sickness. I remember one suffering patient who the nurses felt should have died "days ago." Her grandson was to be married in three weeks, and in that time, the floor of nurses set up the wedding ceremony in her room. She lived the three weeks but died soon after the wedding ceremony that took place in her hospital room.

One of the most difficult things to do is watch a loved one change both physically and psychologically yet accept that there may not be anything a family can do. It is possible that a time will come when you cannot heal your parents. Then there will be a time when, as a caretaker, you accept the inevitability of your loved one's death. In the latter years of our lives, we find ourselves in a new situation: a vocation ends, physical capacities become limited, and loved ones die. In such difficult times, the past has more to offer than the future, and death is always at the door. Old people worry about death, but more so about who will care for them if they become ill or infirm. Illness as a lived experience usually becomes a family matter. An elderly parent facing the everyday problems of how to cope with illness will often turn to his or her children. Some adult children are unprepared for this occurrence, and this is not surprising. One day someone is in total charge of his or her life, career, and family, and then everything changes. Suddenly, a competent parent becomes helpless, and siblings can become indifferent and indecisive. Some families discuss feelings openly, and this helps them put things into perspective. Other families cannot communicate openly, and this makes caregiving much harder. Among all of these families, I found a level of depression and helplessness in caregivers whose elderly parents did not go back to their former independence prior to hospitalization. The caregivers felt they had to do it all and took on the responsibility of providing everything for their parent.

Many adult children expressed their anger because they did not want to "end up like their parents." Their parents, despite serious illness, were not unhappy and had the wisdom to talk about how it felt to be dependent on people.

But because they were grateful for the smallest courtesies from the nursing staff, they never complained because "it might only get worse." Year after year, as patients were discharged quicker and sicker, adult children expressed more anger and stress. If a parent went to a nursing home, adult children complained that they would never want to "end up like this." Caregivers found themselves doing double- and triple-duty for their parents, and many were confronted with "double bind" situations. That is, they were caught between the responsibilities to themselves, those to their families, and those to their parents.

It is important to take time and consider the impact of caretaking, for it can continue for months and sometimes even years. Talking about the commitment may require you to openly discuss it with your family because the decision to become a caregiver directly involves everyone in your life. Most people feel they are unable to perform the work of caregiving simply because previous generations chose not to caretake, sending their loved ones to nursing homes. The stories in this chapter illustrate that families often do not communicate and therefore struggle unnecessarily, underestimating their own power. Just like with Virginia, a harmless remark can cause a burst of feeling from parents and siblings because everyone's sensitivity is heightened to any form of discord within the family. Thus, feelings of resentment and anger can be detrimental to the health of both the caregiver and the care-receiver.

Even well-prepared families agree that caregiving is difficult work, and caregivers sometimes resist treatment for themselves despite being in need of care. As I think back, nothing I have learned in my 28 years of working with families and staff members at the Lahey Clinic has struck me more than a patient and family's need for reassurance and hope. Illness is a terrifying experience for both patient and family. It is important that both parties be able to bolster each other's courage and hope.

3

THE MAN WITH 10,000 NAMES

Acting like a sponge, illness soaks up personal and social significance from the world of the sick person. For the families . . . and for the health professionals who treat them, an acute sensibility to stigma and shame is a necessity. That sensibility is a commitment to what is at stake in the care of the chronically ill: namely a willingness to help bear the burden of the lived experience of suffering.

—Arthur Kleinman, MD, *The Illness Narratives*

Pasquale "Pat" Enrico had a unique approach to dealing with his illness. Being obsessive-compulsive, he would write down the names of people in life, from TV hosts and presidents to neighbors and immigrants in his Italian community, all in an effort to not only remember his previous life but also to come to terms with his illness. His five children described how caretaking truly became a family affair and how they got to know their father through both witnessing his interactions with doctors and reading the list of names he composed. Pat revealed to me his own side of the story as a care-receiver as well, acknowledging his loneliness and fear of abandonment for the first time in his life.

I met Pat in 1979 at the Lahey Clinic Medical Center as he lay in his hospital bed, waiting for prostate surgery. His nurse had referred him to me for emotional support and relaxation therapy because of his high blood pressure. People like Pat often find a hospital admission extremely stressful, and that stress can complicate the medical treatment. Many studies show that emotional problems can cause longer hospital stays. As for Pat, he had seen a therapist several times during his life and had benefited from the therapeutic process. He agreed to meet with me but refused the relaxation tape, instead choosing the rosary beads on his nightstand as a form of relaxation. He preferred rosary beads, prayer beads, and prayer. The first thing he told me was that he had been an active board member of the Danvers State Hospital for many years. He was so animated over this position that I caught the first glimpse of what turned out to be a very special person. Not only did he have a passion for life, but he had overcome many adversities as well. Pat was very talkative and seemed to enjoy conversation; I noticed that he became focused on my name and nationality. When I gave him a card, he asked me to write my name on the back of the card. I also invited him to the support group that I managed, the Prostate Health Support Group. He refused to attend. He enjoyed talking of the past, and because his place of employment, a commercial baking company called Betsy Ross Baking Co., had closed its doors, he was out of work. That day, he asked if I knew about Sacco and Vanzetti—my interest was raised because of his remembrance of the story. One thing was very evident about this man, something that developed early on and became clearer as the years went by: he had a pervasive sense of helplessness, and though he was not hopeless, he was very sad and lonely. The loneliness crept up on him most often when he was with his family, yet he was nurturing to his children and grandchildren and supported many family members financially. He placed considerable demands on them once he retired and became ill. He once confided to me that he was never lonely when he was politically active, such as helping local politicians get elected. Pat had the prostate surgery, but because his tumor was benign, he did not require treatment.

I was not surprised to see him again a year later, this time in our behavioral medicine department, experiencing the symptoms of obsessive compulsive disorder (OCD). OCD involves consistent negative thoughts that interfere with normal thought processes and compulsions, or having strong impulses to lessen the uneasiness that can derive from obsessions. Compulsions often manifest in the patient during their daily activities, making mundane activities, such as brushing one's teeth, more like rituals. Although Pat at first used memorization to compensate for his lack of a primary education, remembering certain facts, names, dates, numbers, states, and politicians, it later became a compulsion. He had a strong desire to perfectly recite and document the names and facts of people in his generation, and most striking was Pat's obsessive fascination with the facts of his earlier life. This included the famous Sacco and Vanzetti case, for politics and Italians were two of his passions.

Pat was an Italian immigrant who had come to the United States and settled in Lawrence, Massachusetts, with his sister, a mill worker, and her family. "We were all crammed into a four room tenement on Elm Street," he remembers. Lawrence was known as "Immigrant City" during the height of the Industrial Revolution, but Pat refused to take a job in a mill on the advice of his sister. "Never work in a mill for those wasps. They squeeze all the oil from your body," she said. Having only a seventh-grade education, Pat said that when he was in school, he was one of the oldest boys in class, so he stopped going to school and therefore he always felt that reading was above his capabilities. However, one thing he was great at all his life was "remembering faces and names."

In 1912, when the Bread and Roses Strike hit Lawrence, he was hidden away by his parents and family members in the attic of the tenement in which they lived. The strike committee decided to evacuate all the children from Lawrence so that they would not starve, sending them to foster homes in

Philadelphia and New York. There were certain things he said he would always remember from that time: The police, who were armed with clubs, were yelling in the hallway, "Where are the rest of those little dagos?"; Pat, five years old, and his sister were huddled alone under a plank floor in a storage room of the tenement. Anna LoPezzi, a striker, was killed early on in the strike, and another striker, Joseph Caruso, was charged with her murder even though the defense produced witnesses who saw a policeman fire several shots at Mrs. LoPezzi. But his most vivid recollection was from 1927, when at the age of 19, he sat with other men in a vacant small house on Elm Street and waited by the radio to hear that Sacco and Vanzetti, both active anarchists fighting for the rights of Italian immigrants, had been electrocuted for a crime "they did not commit." He believed in their innocence with his "whole heart." These names and hundreds of others play a significant role in his life.

He resorted to memorizing people's names, especially those of the train attendants who allowed him to cross the railroad tracks and collect the loose coal dropped by the trains on their way to the station. He resold the coal to people in the neighborhood and began to memorize their names as well. In the later years in which I knew him, he brought a notebook to the hospital with him "in case he needed to remember a name." He asked me to write my name in his notebook and also took my card.

Pat had two stenographers' notebooks in his hospital room, both filled with names of people he had known during his adolescence. He told me that most of the people were dead, and together we counted over 1,000 names. He told me that when he could not remember a date or a piece of history, he would call a long list of people that included everyone from family members to radio stations, libraries, and television stations. No matter what time it was, Pat made his way down the list in order to find out the information.

By 1991, the names were coming faster, and Pat continued to make calls to his family regardless of the hour. By this time he had his wife calling his children or friends as well. If a name he was looking for was not in the telephone book, he would even call friends of friends. His family reported that while asking for a name, he would apologize and cry as if it meant his whole life. If the name given was not correct, or until the correct spelling was provided, he would cry. We had tried talking therapy, medications, and inpatient admissions, but his family was still feeling the burden of Pat's illness. His large family took turns responding to his demands for information, but eventually one of Pat's five children called and told me that this could not go on. By this time he was calling people for the names of hundreds of people, places, and things.

Pat had an extremely large, supportive family. At the scheduled family meeting to discuss Pat's caregiving options, I was not surprised to find all of Pat's children, their spouses, and his grandchildren in attendance. It was the first and last time in my career that I would address every single family member of the elderly patient, discussing their options for care. Pat's family was unique, and I had never met a family so invested in their father's well-being.

At that meeting, Pat announced that he wanted to receive shock treatments because an Italian doctor had invented it, and he had witnessed patients improve at the Danvers hospital where he had served on the board of directors for many years. He reported that during his tenure at this mental hospital, he and a highly respected woman who also sat on the board had managed to stop the treatment of "washing down patients with a hose." He sat with his children, crying because he felt he was making them unhappy. At this point, the only care the family could provide was their presence, but it was not until the doctor, Dr. McLaughlin, entered the room to evaluate Pat that his family really understood who their father was and what his real illness was.

Pat reported that he had been mostly alone from the age of five and that he had had no relationship with his father. The psychiatrist asked, "Well, Pat, what did you do with your father?" "Nothing, never," answered Pat. Pat's hazel eyes turned glassy and started to tear. "Who took care of you?" I asked. "I took care of myself," he said. His children wept openly as he talked about how his parents left him and his two siblings in a locked apartment from 6:00 AM to 3:00 PM when they went out to work every day. His father died in Italy when the local mafia robbed him at gunpoint for refusing to pay for his own protection. Pat did not return to Italy for the funeral. "For this reason," he said, "I have fought for justice and truth for Italian Americans, [lived] through the depression, great wars, and [fought for] Sacco & Vanzetti, who I believe were innocent." Dr. McLaughlin seemed to be interested in the two anarchists of Italian decent who were electrocuted on August 23, 1927, and as he asked more questions, Pat's children seemed disinterested. They had heard it before. The most riveting detail that seemed very important to Pat was that Justice Felix Frankfurter and his wife Marion had supported Sacco and Vanzetti. Dr. McLaughlin was familiar with the article written by Felix Frankfurter in the *Atlantic Monthly*. The next question stunned us all: "Can you remember your most exciting time?" the psychologist asked. Without hesitation, Pat said, "The movie *Yankee Doodle Dandy* because James Cagney was singing and dancing, and his mother and father were there." With his whole life in review, this movie was key to his loneliness and sense of loss, and after he talked about this, Pat came up with his astounding request: "I've decided to have shock treatments," he said. "I'm ashamed and embarrassed causing all of you such worry and pain, especially your mother. I want the names to stop. I don't want to call anyone anymore, but I can't stop them from coming into my head. I need shock treatments." There was fire in this message for this family. They all seemed stunned, though I suspected some of them knew this was coming. Elizabeth's mouth began to twitch, an unconscious habit that arose when she felt overwhelmed. Pat had not mentioned this to her before.

Tony, one of Pat's sons, spoke first. "Well, Ernest Hemingway had shock treatments at the Mayo Clinic. After a while he convinced his doctors to stop because he thought it would ruin his mind. Then he went home and shot himself." Lisa chirped in that author Sherwin Nuland wrote of his own experience with mental illness and shock therapy. He feared losing his sanity, and the shock treatments "helped him." This was a way for the children to convince themselves to bow to their father's wishes. Pat's wife of over 50 years was skeptical that shock treatments would bring about a miracle or that improvement would happen with shock treatments, but the children convinced her that it was a necessity. Pat sat with his children, crying still because he felt he was causing them so much trouble.

Tony said that Dr. McLaughlin had taught him more about his father's history than he had learned in his own 59 years of questions, and he read Pat's psychiatrist's report aloud. "Your father is not demented, and I doubt he has Alzheimer's. He is depressed, and I will recommend psychotherapy and ECT." The family was happy to hear that he did not have Alzheimer's disease but were overwhelmed at the thought of electroshock treatments. They all seemed stunned.

Pat's decision to undergo ECT (electroconvulsive therapy) greatly affected all of Pat's children, especially his daughter Geraldine and his son Pat. "My whole body ached after watching the video on ECT. I had a tingling in my arm and was so scared I was having stroke afterwards that I went to the ER," Geraldine told me.

Pat's son recounts the feeling of entering the hospital before his father was to undergo ECT:

> Outside it looks like a beautiful French country house. The entrance was large and spacious with a white fence. Inside, the entry had a barricade made of steel, oh my God . . . even the elevators were locked until someone opened them. By the time we headed to the interview room, I forgot I was locked in. It was actually kind of serene and peaceful. There wasn't any yelling. There were many old people here, walking and talking, lots of young people also . . . I was feeling bewildered, scared, maybe like my father . . . frightened of fear itself. My father knows what he's doing and I have to respect his wishes. I still question myself, though. Should I, as the oldest son, step in and say no? But no to what? My father, my mom, everybody. We just couldn't go on like this. All I could do was just put one foot in front of the other and hope the treatments worked.

On the first day of his ECT treatments, Pat told Geraldine, "All I wanted was to be like everyone else—why me?" With his face covered in tears, he asked if she would visit and begged her not to abandon him. Geraldine told me afterward that she began getting upset over things that had never bothered her before. She said, "When I packed my father's clothes to bring here, they weren't even new. Father's Day was just last Sunday. Couldn't my siblings buy him new things to bring to the hospital? My Mom hadn't cooked any food for him either." She recognized this was not her usual style with her family, and the stresses and strains were affecting everyone in the family, except Lucy, Pat's wife of 50 years. Caregivers like Geraldine, who usually take on the lion's share of responsibilities, have expressed this feeling many times. Geraldine was able to see this as it was, and her anger seemed to be directed toward her mother. It was hard for her to understand that her mother had silently, for years, kept everything under control, not wanting to disturb their lives.

In the weeks that followed, Lucy reluctantly decided that she would concentrate on caring for herself during her husband's hospitalization, and she visited him only once. Although his children and grandchildren visited him daily, Lucy silently feared the rest of her life. As she took on more of the responsibility in taking care of Pat, she became more insensitive to his feelings. Her family expressed guilt and anger toward her because they wanted her to have a more active role in caring for their father, her husband. "She keeps telling me she is tired, but so am I," remarked a daughter.

I realized that although Pat was at the head of this family, his wife was really at its heart. In my research, I found that many Italian women yielded authority to their husbands while assuming control of the emotional, nurturing, and domestic part of their lives. Lucy, however, was a very modern, second-generation Italian woman who had completed high school. Although Pat yielded authority to his employers and politicians, Lucy yielded authority to no one.

I decided to shift focus within the family to provide more support for Lucy to preserve the family's traditions and strengths. Lucy was simply overwhelmed. Clearly she had proved her resourcefulness for caring for Pat and his OCD tendencies for many years, and her caregiving skills were fully honed. She was just tired, and she later told me that for two weeks she was just devoid of energy. This is not unusual when caregiving continues for a prolonged period of time.

There were times when I had concerns about symbiotic family loyalty, which occurs when people become too emotionally involved during caregiving. The family was in close union with each other and lived in close proximity to each other, but they also showed that they were emotionally independent and lived their own lives. Several meetings with the family convinced me that in spite of the caretaking challenges each one faced, they were still able to go on with their own lives. They were committed to the caregiving of their father and were loyal to each other in spite of their differences because everyone's focus was on caregiving. Feeling closeness to one's family is one of the most powerful human motivations. This family was very loyal to each other and remained committed to sharing caretaking responsibilities for 20 years; even the grandchildren became involved. Often it was just a phone call or a quick visit after work; any form of contact gives the care-receiver the motivation and reassurance to continue through the day.

After the first inpatient ECT treatment, Pat received ECT two to three times a week for six weeks. I visited him once a week, and he was anxious before treatment and very lethargic afterward. I put a new stenographer's notebook on the table next to Pat's bed, and he instructed even those who were not family to write a few words in the notebook. His friend Patsy simply wrote, "Patsy Amante was here."

Pat seemed to experience an immediate and powerful recovery. Everyone relaxed. His obsession with names dissipated. Challenges for the caregiving family turned into opportunities for including him in everyday activities, and this gave him a chance to tell his family the many stories he had stored. For weeks and months at a time, he was back to himself, until his next shock treatment was needed. Instead of repeating names and dates, Pat always repeated, "The only thing we have to fear is fear itself." The irony was that Pat had been fearful his whole life, from the childhood and adolescent scars that had never healed, and eventually this had led to depression and the resulting OCD.

Often patients it hard to come to terms with how they imagined they would deal with their sickness and how they actually dealt with it once it was upon them. Pat expressed his OCD, but as an illustration of his depression. His illness was not repressed, and instead, he was able to share his grief and fear of abandonment with his family. His OCD, depression, and ECT treatments, along with his determination not to create family turmoil, were extremely stressful for him.

Caretakers, on the other hand, fear illness, and that fear prevents them from preemptively making plans for times of illness and death. Although there were five adult children to tend to Pat's needs, when they got overwhelmed, they were able to turn to outside support, such as religious support groups, psychotherapy, and talking therapy to cope with the stresses of caretaking. Even though Pat's illness (his OCD) began slowly, he and his family had many years to reflect and try to prepare for what the future would bring. When he asked for ECT treatments, his family was distressed but accepted his wish.

Pat took his whole family on his care-receiving journey. For over 25 years, they were his caregivers. I became the person they could call for advice and support. Once he was released from the hospital after completing ECT, Pat's mantra was "I will try and do it myself." He eventually had to have daily help in the home, and his wife became exhausted from the 24-hour responsibility. She had to get out every weekend and socialize with friends. Their children called him daily, and one of them visited after work. Every person in the family contributed to his care in one way or another.

For Pat, like many of the Americans of Italian descent who accepted these hardships, prejudices, and put-downs, certain habits became what the dictionary defines as a compulsion, an "irresistible urge" like an addiction that he could not help. Despite the complexity of Pat's diagnosis, there was no mystery about "his names." He told everyone he met about them. I knew Pat and his family many years before he died, and he shared his "name finding" even as his family tried many approaches to help him, and I myself struggled through many months with them. I became my own expert on the Sacco and Vanzetti case, which took place when, like today, times were difficult; bombings, wars, assassinations, and great changes were taking place as our country entered the 20th century. Pat challenged me more than any other patient, and I found myself bringing up his story in my own supervision and therapy. Were these names an expression of the depression? Was the constant focus on Immigrant City, Sacco and Vanzetti, and all of the other names his way of getting attention as his social circle grew smaller, and the people in his life disappeared?

For many years I puzzled over what these names, which were painstakingly descriptive, meant to this man. One day he told me. Remembering names, he said, began when he was locked up in his apartment while his parents went to work. He was not allowed to open the door unless he knew the name of the person knocking. This seemed to be a clue, and as I pressed further, went over some of his records, and spoke to his wife about it, I found that on the night of their honeymoon (probably as a defense against feelings of inadequacy), he locked himself in the closet so that they would not have to go out. The couple never told anyone, and his symptoms of fear disappeared until he was let go from a job he had held for 35 years with no insurance or severance pay. One morning he awoke and had dreamed he was sent to jail with Sacco and Vanzetti, and the names began to appear again. The names represented an Italian community that he loved and cherished for his whole life. Most of the people were now gone or had moved to another part of the city. His political activity was a shield because Sacco and Vanzetti and many like them went underground to help their own. He hated the mafia, and though he enjoyed watching movies such as *The Godfather,* he told me that he had spent all of his life as an American proud of his heritage—without stint or reservation—and he loved this country, its agonies, and it triumphs, and his Italian heritage dedicated him to his country. For me this was the real authentic Italian American story that has never been told. As his life became organized around his compulsion, his family focused only on his "sickness." One day many years later, his daughter and I visited the memorial bas-relief of Sacco and Vanzetti designed by the sculptor Gutzon Borglum at the Boston Public Library. It reads,

> What I wish more than all in this last hour of agony is that our case and our fate may be understood in their real being and serve as a tremendous lesson to the forces of freedom so that our suffering and death will not have been in vain.

The end came peacefully for Pat at the age of 86. An article in the local paper after the funeral read, "So many people came to pay their respects the line went on for several blocks. An entourage of state troopers was needed to accompany his casket to the burial." His daughter repeated, at graveside, an epitaph from "The Little Prince" by Debussy. "My father was a prince," she said. "He would say 'When I am gone, you will look into the sky, and you will see me as a star. I will be laughing and singing.' My father," she said, "could have been the world's best singer. For now, for me, he is the world's best star in the heavens. When I look up each night, I can hear him laughing and singing." Although Pat did not deny any of his emotions, he was one of the most vulnerable people I worked with. Whenever he talked about himself, he always cried. He was a simple and genuine human being. He was a real Yankee Doodle Dandy of his time. I liked to think that like many other Italian Americans of his generation, he was the carrier of ideals, a man who tried to make the world a more beautiful place for all who came after him.

4

ATTACHMENT BEHAVIOR
IN ADULT LIFE

Intimate attachments to other human beings are the hub around which a person's life revolves, not only when he is an infant or a toddler or a schoolchild, but throughout his years of maturity and into old age . . . attachment behavior is an extremely important survival mechanism elicited by the circumstances of the time.

—John Bowlby, 1969, Tavistock Clinic of Human Relations,
London, England

For most individuals, the bond between a child and his or her parents continues through adult life. During childhood, a child's attachment to specific nurturing persons (often a parent or a caregiver or nanny is essential for a child's well-being and emotional growth. During healthy adolescence and adulthood and into old age, this bond persists, and new bonds are formed. In childhood the mother, father, or significant caregiver is the attachment figure, whereas in old age the principle figure is usually an adult child. When an aging adult has no children, a relative such as a niece, nephew, sister, or cousin can be this figure. Usually the attachment figure is related by either blood or marriage, but if no relative is available, a friend can be substituted. If all adult members of a family are deceased, the attachment behavior is directed to members of younger generations, usually grandchildren. Attachment behavior is a better basis for bonding in adult life than the obvious alternative of sexual desire. Once the attachment behavior becomes established, it is very persistent and resists extinction, whereas sexual desire is sometimes persistent and sometimes not. These connections are unique for each individual and are irreplaceable. We suffer greatly once the deep bond of attachment is severed.

Weiss (1982) and other theorists inspired by Bowlby have reported that attachment in children contributes to children's keeping close to protective adults In our society we all have the priviledge of choosing who we want to associate with. Weiss argues that adults establish bonds to other adults that are, in essential respects, identical to the attachment that children make to primary caretakers. These appear only in relationships of central emotional importance. In Caregiving and caretaking behavior has been established in childhood and this behavior is highly persistent and resists extinction, sexual desire on the other hand is sometimes persistent and sometimes not. . . . Insofar as attachment is reciprocated it provides a better basis for caregiving and caretaking.

Weiss reports that there are three criteria of attachment: (1) that the person wants to be with the attachment figure, especially when he is under stress; (2) that he derives comfort and security from the attachment figure; and (3) that he protests when the attachment figure becomes or threatens to become inaccessible. Attachment behavior in adult life, with all its variations, is a straightforward continuation of attachment behavior that occurs in childhood. Though human behavior is variable and there are great cultural differences, certain patterns in attachment behavior are common. In extreme danger we feel restless, insecure, and sometimes terrified. In sickness and calamity or conditions of sudden danger, or when we appraise a situation as dangerous, attachment behavior is more readily elicited.

Most of us would choose to be with someone who is stronger, wiser, and more helpful when we get sick. With few exceptions, we all have experienced this filial devotion from someone at some point in our lives. To some extent, humans are always scanning people they love for predictable behavior. An attachment figure is someone who will be faithful, steadfast, and available when you need that person. In old age or at times of crisis or illness, we summon up this behavior and look for support and nurturance from people who matter to us. Having someone stand beside you when you are vulnerable provides an inner feeling of security and the confidence to face whatever comes up. Knowing that this attachment figure is accessible is a source of psychological sustenance; it is the nourishment that gives meaning to life and the motivation to keep going. Though friends and neighbors can offer support and the necessities of life, only within the relative kinship or close friendship can continuing assistance be expected whether or not there is reciprocal devotion.

Adult children love their parents, and some bend over backwards in order to help them deal with the complexities of aging, chronic illness, or disability. Others just distract themselves and their parents by not talking about what their fears and needs are and then cut off all further conversation by saying, "Don't worry, you will be just fine." In some families, talking about illness or dying is taboo. One woman confided to me that if she brought up the subject of illness or dying, her mother, who was very superstitious, would think that it might happen. Her mother was a controlling and bitter woman all her life. It may appear as if the mother was "protecting" her daughter, from dealing with the possibility of her own death, but a closer look shows that, in fact, the mother placed a greater burden on her daughter. Over the long years of caregiving for her mother, who eventually became demented and physically limited, this daughter had internalized her mother's conflicts, resentments, and superstitions. She finally sought treatment and realized that her mother's anger and low self-esteem had nothing to do with her. As a result, the bond with her deceased mother was not broken, and she learned how to nurture herself, something her mother had never done for herself.

Caregivers who are caught up in this situation build a one-sided picture of their loved one so that they can shut off all conscious processes of feelings of anger and frustration in order to stay in control. In other situations, consciously or unconsciously, some caregivers are held together merely by an idealized image of a loved one. In shutting off feelings of anger or frustration that he may have against the parent who expects too much, a caregiver will be prevented from living his own life. In such a state, a person is naturally liable to influences that can paralyze any action and cause cynicism. A caregiver becomes entangled in an emotional web, as one denial leads to another one and so on. In many of these families, where there is a blind spot about keeping conflicts from awareness, there is a great deal of rationalization, which can lead to a numbness to the emotional experience of attachment.

Denying and fearing that at some time in your life you will become a caregiver is not the answer and may prevent you from seeing your parent's condition as it really is. Thinking about caretaking may bring up resentments about the ways in which your parents failed you. Hundreds of feelings and reactions are common, but they do not mean you cannot be a caregiver. The worst part about fear and denial is that you miss the opportunity to communicate with your loved ones, and when they get sick, it may be too late. Attachment caregiving is what connects the self to society, and this connection persists throughout life. In my research with adult children and elderly parents, the adult children who took on the caregiving role said that they felt helpless, hopeless, and, to some extent, depressed.

Most adult children said they were not prepared to take on the caregiving role. Some said that there were dramatic shifts in family roles. One daughter arranged for her teenager to do all the grocery shopping for her family, and her husband pitched in with other duties, which then interfered with the many functions in his work. Adult children in my research were fearful that they could not fulfill both filial obligations and these new responsibilities within their own families. Once they realized that they were not alone, and that help was available, caregiving became an opportunity for them to grow within their own families. Even where relationships are stretched beyond limits, it is possible that adult children have, within themselves, the confidence that comes from attachment in childhood to navigate a new passage in life called caregiving.

Negative forecasts of how an elderly parent will act when she is ill have caused many adult children to predict that caregiving will be a burden and will lead to burnout not only for them but for their families as well. Many times I have heard variations of "The golden years suck" repeated by adult children whose parents are in a state of decline. Freud's profoundly important discovery that fear can arise not only from a forecast of how the external world and the people in it may behave but also from forecasts of how we ourselves may possibly act is very relevant here. Thus, seeing ourselves negatively in others can produce fear reactions that profoundly affect the way look at caregiving.

Knowing that an attachment figure is reachable and responsive gives someone who is ill a strong sense of security. Bowlby describes this security as a good insurance policy "whatever our age." When an aging person feels protected, comfortable, and secure, he is able to take part in various activities with his peers. This is a basic component of feeling secure, provided of course that the attachment figure can be accessible and will be responsive when needed. In families where caregiving arrangements are somewhat stable, the pattern of attachment behavior between caretaker and child, once established, tends to persist and does not change. In adulthood and old age, the changing of roles is common and constantly updated even though there is a time lag. If the role is reversed, and an adult child becomes the parent, and the parent becomes the child, it becomes a pathological relationship. This could mean that those roles were never corrected or updated. But it could also mean that a vicious circle is set in motion because the caregiver sees the situation as a merciless battle, and in order to attain peace and harmony within the attachment relationship, the caregiver submits to this abnormal behavior. It may be the only approach because the caregiver has become detached from the adult parent. As long as the caregiver can keep this emotional distance, he feels safe. But this is no true solution because the compulsive craving for closeness of attachment behavior brings to an end the internal calm and tranquility that is required. The care-receiver, on the other hand, is not dead and is aware of impending loss. Under this internal stress, whether real or imagined, the sick parent alienates herself and others. When an elderly person loses the bonds of attachment, she suffers a deep and pungent distress. Nothing is as important as understanding the process of attachment behavior in caretaking, and because it is often an internal process, it is not always visible. For a harmonious relationship, caregiver and care-receiver must be aware of each other's point of view, feelings, goals, and intentions. An open and free communication and dialogue can enable the caregiver to recognize that the negative images of childhood may interfere with what he may want to do for a loved one. The goal in caregiving is different for those who believe that there is something inherent, worthwhile, and good in human nature. Redefined, reinforced, and directed by such elements as will, faith, and reason with one's religious or ethical concept of attachment in caregiving, we see better possibilities and not only a moral obligation but also a moral privilege. Once we can appreciate attachment behavior, a new light is thrown on the caregiving and care-receiving process.

Even when growing up in unfavorable conditions, such as having the loss of a parent or an unavailable significant caregiver, it is still possible to overcome this adversity and find an attachment figure in the environment. In hospitals, nursing homes, and retirement homes, people become friends because there is a shared environment that brings people together in special relationships with a cast of characters much like themselves. Though making new affiliations in such environments takes a while, it is possible to form a tie with a friend that resembles the attachment relationship.

Enduring the impact of an estranged or lost relationship that was once valued can cause people to be so enraged that they deny a family member ever existed. Internally, the moods and rages are like a roller coaster; such a woman was Agnes, who experienced these moods and rages. A care attendant brought her to the emergency room when she fell down a flight of stairs. Agnes, aged 82, was unable to return to her own home and asked to go to a nursing home. Her husband had died four and a half years before, and since then she had been depressed and despondent and neglected her personal care. She was somewhat unkempt, but otherwise alert and oriented. She said she did not have any children, even though an old record revealed two adult children. She never had any visitors, and the nurses reported she told them she had no family. Several days later, the police revealed that her children had reported her missing. With a superficial reconciliation established with her children, Agnes was able to go to the nursing home of her choice. When I met with her children, they told me that the only contact they had had with their mother since their father died was a card at Christmas. Agnes changed her will, told her children that they would not be included in the inheritance, and refused to tell her children who would. She did not get along with her daughter-in-law and felt that her son did not devote enough time to her. The mother's rage at her children was never resolved, and even after brief therapy with her family, she remained bitter and resentful. In the end, when she died, the children told me that they were equal beneficiaries of the inheritance. The grandson, however, who was cared for by Agnes in his childhood, had emotional problems when his grandmother died and was referred for counseling.

In this family, the attachment bond was severed over money. But was it really? Based on what happened to Agnes's grandson after she died, it can be implied that attachments can have other subsystems that affect caregivers situations and that a grandchild is under a great deal of stress when the relationship with a grandparent is divided. Should the children have known that the mother's behavior was caused by rage that they were not giving her the attention she thought she deserved? This is hard to know, but in my experience, when it comes to money, the closest families find themselves dealing with emotional injury, rage, and narcissistic hurts.

At the same time, I have witnessed extraordinary recovery from a loss of a close attachment figure. Widows, for instance, report despair, protest, detachment, disbelief, and a tendency to hope for a reunion when a spouse dies. Many widows and widowers find a new supply of physical energy when they find attachment substitutes and are able to both love and experience being loved again. It is not only the young child who is pliable; all of us have within ourselves the capacity to change because attachment behavior is so vital. It is natural for human beings to share and find joy and satisfaction while trying to understand each other.

Having someone stand beside you when you are sick gives you the confidence to make bonds with those who care for you, especially those people other than your family. We grow up looking for these relationships during adolescence, in adulthood, and straight through to old age. The story of "The Man with 10,000 Names," in Chapter 3, shows how attachment figures become available during the life cycle. When people and networks were not available, Pat Enrico had started making a list of names of all the people who meant something to him. In many ways, this list represented the attachments he had made during his lifetime. He said he felt comfortable and secure with, and felt a shared sense of trust with, most of the people in his lists. Some were enemies or people who did him wrong, and after he wrote those names down, he said he "just forgot about them." When I asked him why the name of President Roosevelt's secretary of state was so important to him, he said, "I trusted he would get us out of the Depression of the 1930s." The search for these figures and the list-making started once he was let go from his job and then got sick. In his world he understood that he had very strong support from his family; nevertheless, these figures and his list-making were remnants of the severed attachment he suffered in childhood.

The main feature of an attachment relationship in caregiving and care-receiving in old age is that it has the capacity to sustain both individuals. Most people are resilient and much stronger than we suspect. While working with people, I found that caretakers and caregivers were capable of great courage and empathy, but not while in isolation. What was most essential was a link to people who were informed and prepared. Though we can never be fully prepared when the crisis comes, the intrinsic forces of attachment behavior are within oneself. This force cannot be taught, but given a chance, its potentialities can develop. For an ill parent or loved one, life can seem empty and can have no meaning when attachment figures, family, friends, and relatives lose interest and withdraw affection.

When we lose someone who is an attachment figure, we remain inconsolable. Expressions of sorrow when a loved one withdraws affection or is lost include weeping, feelings of helplessness, fear, criticizing a loved one, and an appeal to others for help. Some people cannot express these feelings because they fear that expressing them would be a form of weakness or begging for help. Of those I worked with who were alienated from their family, many overcame obstacles once they became reunited and worked hard to have a rapport with one another. Good fortune also seemed to smile upon them, and they were more hopeful instead of giving in to despair. Others, where a positive relationship never existed and the individual behaved like a doormat (someone who does not protest or express anger or rage) and refused any reconciliation, were more likely to be abandoned by those they loved most. If no attachment figures were available, many of the patients substituted another person or paid help. In each relationship it is clear that an attachment figure provided not only an emotional and physical role, but also much hope.

There may be no time to find a substitute in old age as there was in childhood. People try harder when they know they are supported. We are all our happiest when someone comes to our aid.

Having a trusted person on your team when you are faced with serious conditions, such as illness and danger, is what really matters. In caretaking, an attachment figure is the person most people turn to in situations of illness, sorrow, and grief. Without this relationship, and with unmet needs, old people can remain inconsolable. Acknowledging that eventually, within our lifetime, there may be a period of caregiving for an older person does not mean accepting a glum future: rather, it involves developing a deeper appreciation of what is truly meaningful in our lives. A caregiver is usually brought into the uncertain and fearful world of pain and disability. As a result of these experiences, certain anxieties arise that can choke off any recognition of one's own needs. The care-receiver also has the same anxieties and the urgent need to be cared for. For example, Philip, a 73-year-old retired automobile salesman, describes his visit to the diabetic clinic:

> Frankly, it is just too much. My eyesight is failing, and they told me that it's because I am not keeping my sugar under control. I am a sick man, but everyone blames me for my dependency and my bad behavior. The diabetic nurse gave me a chart to write down everything I eat for a week. I cannot see the paper, so I have to call my son to enlarge it on a copy machine. My wife takes the other list to the grocery store, and now she thinks she must control my diabetes by cooking and giving me controlled portions. She gets upset at me while doing the cooking, saying, "What will you do if something happens to me?" At Thanksgiving last year, she made a sugar-free pudding cake, but I am easily seduced by desserts, so I ate the pecan pie and ice cream. Nothing makes me feel worse than when my daughter says, "You might think about others when you do things like eating pecan pie." I want to be like everyone else. Everyone is telling me how to run my life. More exercise every day, watch my diet, don't cut my own nails, drink water, and eliminate potassium in my diet. I do the best I can, but as I said, it is just too much. When I register high blood sugars and relapse, they say I brought [it] on myself because I did not do enough or I did too much. It is a no-win situation.

Philip's son, Philip Jr. (a lawyer), comments on the effects his father has on him, when his father has periods of disorientation or reacts to suggestions with anger and criticism.

> Our family has always been somewhat dysfunctional. Dad is very authoritarian, and sometimes he seems to treat my mother like a housekeeper. She, on the other hand, doesn't tell him this, and when it gets too much, she wants my sister and me to take over things like shopping and talking to Father about his aggressive behavior. He does not drive, and she has become his chauffeur, and last year she had an accident. My father is pretty self-involved. It has always been this way, but his illness has just made it clearer to us. It is partly our fault because when he does not follow the treatment program, we do not confront him. My mother, on the other hand, is in good health, but she looks at least 15 years older, and she is really slowing up. It is [an] impossible situation. I worry about my father, and my mother is wearing herself out. She tells me constantly, "I will die before your father."

Philip Sr. was grieving not only the loss of good health but also the loss of stature in his family. Giving up his driver's license forced on him the realization that he was becoming dependent and may someday be totally dependent on others. Prior to the diabetes, the only people he depended on were his customers. It was not death that concerned him; it was his progression into becoming an invalid. He felt guilty that he had put "this burden" on his family. He and his wife had looked forward to retirement and going to Florida. Phillip Sr. said he could not talk openly to his wife and children about his fear of dying "like his mother," who had also had diabetes. His father had died a lingering death, and he said, "I will not get better, and I do not want to die like him." This man who had great pride in his appearance began neglecting himself. His wife, on the other hand, after all that shopping, cleaning, and cooking, turned into a whiny dependent woman when she spoke to her children.

Philip Sr.'s preoccupation with becoming an invalid and becoming dependent on others is one important reason for patients like Philip to have attachment figures in their life. The fear of becoming dependent on others and giving up can only exacerbate any illness. In Philip Sr.'s situation, his chronic illness was not acutely life-threatening. His wife, an independent and younger woman, was very vibrant, and because of this, he felt that he would alienate her if he spoke the truth. He was afraid of losing her to someone else. He revealed that growing up in a family in which his parents had suffered from chronic illness had left a scar on him, and now he was doing the same thing to those he loved most.

In his book *The Illness Narratives,* Arthur Kleinman envisions in "chronic illness and its therapy a symbolic bridge that connects body, self and society . . . we are privileged to discover powers within and between us than can either amplify suffering and disability or dampen symptoms and therefore contribute to care something derived from an earlier phase of life, perhaps one that served a different function"—for example, an adult child feeding the old.

When the elderly parent faces an illness; the attachment to an adult child or relative furnishes a source of sustenance, a meaning to life, and often a motivation to keep going. Only with relatives, kinship, or friends can continuing assistance be expected whether or not there is reciprocal devotion. For adult children or relatives, caregiving is an opportunity to nurture someone who has taken care of them. For many it permits the development of pooled information and a shared exchange of ideas and guidance. Everyone appreciates having someone who is trustworthy and who will stand beside him or her and come to his or her aid in times of illness.

While in good health, many older people like periods of solitude, and some even view it with a sense of relief. In times of illness and old age, however, the attachment figure (often an adult child or relative) becomes the caretaker, and there are times when those treasured moments of solitude are put aside because of time constraints. Those special times cannot be retrieved, so one must make time for moments of solitude and hold on to them. In the beginning of this chapter, I said that once attachment behavior becomes established, it resists extinction. Those moments of solitude are essential for the caregiver who feels isolated from the attachment figures of his life. Recognizing such failures in childhood and giving oneself credit for not having been entirely crushed by earlier circumstances in life gives one freedom and strength to go on.

Though there can be many variations in the ways families may change, divide, and reform, with few exceptions, individuals spend their whole life in close communication with family, friends, and relatives. Weiss reports that those who display behaviors such as attachment are more likely to survive and have descendants in successive generations who also demonstrate such behaviors. Weiss also reports that lifetime relationships offer "a sense of reliable alliance, social integration, being from part of a community of friends, reassurance of worth and an opportunity for nurturance." What an individual who is growing old wants is not money or instrumental services, but love, concern, care, continued contact, advice, reassurance of worth, and the knowledge that she will not be abandoned Sometimes the attachment behavior may consist of no more than checking on the caretaker by eye or ear, by a visit or a telephone call. Often strangeness, fatigue, frights, and the unavailability of the loved one exacerbate the attachment behavior of an ill parent. A clinical illustration may be useful here:

An elderly mother waits for her son after placing a telephone call to his office saying she feels "dizzy." She refuses to call the doctor until her son arrives. In turn her son, feeling stressed, may be angry at her manipulation. He tells her so, and she starts drinking water and crying. It is possible that his mother may have been trying to solve her problem by returning to a form of behavior that was successful during her immature years. It is also possible that the mother's drinking is a result of dryness of the throat, which is a consequence of fear response. I mention this example because often the situation appears as a crisis when it is not, and then action is taken, and an ambulance is called. But let us say that his mother turns out not to need a hospital admission, and the son then appraises the situation as his mother only "seeking attention"—if a conversation later takes place with both mother and son expressing their true feelings, much of the anger felt by the son will be avoided.

Getting angry with an elderly parent gets you nowhere. In the previous situation the mother was contributing to her own isolation and fear. Her son, on the other hand, once he decided to talk to his mother, shifted gears from angry assertions to thoughtful awareness of her fear. When the mother realized how her behavior affected her son and that he would never abandon her, she became less fearful of being alone and less insecure. Her son continued struggling with caregiving and eventually hired a personal care attendant who visited once a week. This example of attachment behavior, in spite of many obstacles, strengthens its value and worth.

We often take for granted that, to some extent, we can tell how our loved ones feel by facial expressions, posture, tone of voice, or actions. No doubt, some of us are more accurate than others. In some cases we may make a prediction of a parent's behavior because over a long period of time, he or she has been consistent, and the situation has never changed. These sorts of observations by an adult child of an aging ill parent, without a conversation, always present a dilemma. An ill parent who feels closeness to a caregiver craves information about that person. It is a way of seeking intimacy and attachment.

In sickness, calamity, and crisis, adults often become demanding of others, and in conditions of sudden danger, a person will almost certainly seek proximity to another known and trusted person. In caregiving, the care-receiver often has an increased attachment to his adult children. It is not regressive. It is a complementary relationship where, during the ordinary course of events, the behavior of one complements the other. An ill, elderly parent in a hospital receives clues from all around him by observing. This observation is learned throughout life and is a simple way to assess danger and avoid it. One of Freud's profoundly important discoveries was that fear can arise not only from forecasts of how the external world and people in it may behave, but also from forecasts of we ourselves may possibly act. Thus, the daughter, by seeing herself negatively in her mother, will produce her own fear reaction. A fear reaction can prevent a daughter or a son from acting as a comforter or protector.

In old age, when attachment behavior can no longer be directed toward members of the family (their deceased children or peers), the attachment behavior is directed to members of a younger generation—grandchildren, nieces, nephews, or familiar friends. Attachment behavior is really vital in the life of humans from the cradle to the grave.

Society has seemingly reinvented itself, and ageism has thrived, and the result is that we question our first bonds of love. Attachment behavior has been adapted not only for the survival of families, but for survival of our species as well. The relationship between an adult child and elderly parent from the earliest years takes form and has meaning because of our interactions in our surroundings and environment. This, in turn, helps us to predict and maneuver to defeat the dangers that come to us during our middle and elderly years. This is common knowledge to our society, and each one of us has a unique personal history and experience. In childhood, we discover how we can ward off frightening things. We also learn to control this behavior throughout the whole life span. I am suggesting, then, that adult children mean comfort and safety to the elderly parent who is ill. When caregivers are experiencing burnout or stress in the crucial relationship at the end of someone's life, nothing seems to make sense. If the world becomes meaningless, one faces a crisis in faith and often bitterness fraught with helplessness and hopelessness.

Older people tend to be more introspective. This is probably because they are aware that death is near. This awareness, in turn, asks us to look at a new meaning to one's life in old age. This involves a community of people who think alike—to think about now, not yesterday, not tomorrow. Victor Frankel states,

Only under the threat and pressure of death does it make sense to do what we can and show, right now. That is, to make proper use of the moment's offer of a meaning to fulfill—be it a deed to do, or work to create, anything to enjoy, or a period of inescapable suffering to go through with courage and dignity . . . Live as if you were living for the second time—and as if you had acted the first time as wrongly as you are about to act now. Once an individual really puts himself into this imagined situation, he will instantaneously become conscious of the full gravity of the responsibility that every person bears throughout every moment of his life—the responsibility for what he will make of the next hour, for how he will shape the next day.

Reflect, but not in silence, in this mirror of the rescuer. Our integrity depends on this. Because middle age is a template for the next generation's creative transformation, there must be a positive experience of positive attachment. If this does not happen, we will have—instead of strength, relatedness, acceptance of old and prior traditions, and values—the hatred of reality. This will be clear: as clear as the reflection in the present-day mirror of an aging population.

The literature supports the theory that the first attachment figure is essential for the growing child's mental health as well as scant attention to the importance to the relationship of attachment to the adult child and aging parent. Bowlby (1969, 1973, 1982), Balint (1965, 1968), and Weiss say repeatedly that this same attachment behavior, though different, is essential and important and perceived as a source of strength to an aging person. Weiss reported, "Attachment in adults is clearly a better basis for a reliable pair bond."

LONG-DISTANCE CAREGIVING AND ATTACHMENT

The long-distance caregiver has her own unique issues. Though attachment behavior is similar to the behavior shown by families who live in close proximity to a care-receiver, the emotional drain of being too far from a loved one when help is needed is devastating. Finding ways to cope is challenging because of the need to depend on others who are in the same locality as a loved one. The result sometimes is that the caregiver may scatter his energies in too many directions. The degree of suffering, of course, varies, but chances are, with an attachment figure such as a spouse or relative to offer support and nurturance, the pain is shared. Besides the feelings of guilt, anger, frustration, and isolation experienced by long-distance caregivers, waiting for the telephone call (that may bring bad news) every day and not knowing when it will come is overwhelming. Other issues include keeping other family members updated and involved with the decision-making process. A study by MetLife found that both primary and secondary long-distance caregivers reported living an average distance of 450 miles away from a loved one. A majority of long-distance caregivers visit at least a few hours a month and spend an average of $392 a month on travel. The most trying aspect of long-distance care giving is the loss of control one feels every day.

When we recognize the role of attachment behavior in later life, we can welcome the new stage in life called caregiving. We will also have a more accurate understanding of why an optimistic, untiring striving toward better ways of caring and toward deeper spiritual knowledge and toward better ways of successful caregiving. After all at some time in our lives, we wish for our older parents to be healthy, happy, and self relient. If we succeed, the rewards are great; but for those who fail, the pain of frustration, shame guilt and anxiety may be severe. Caregiving is an opportunity for nurturing another person, particularly for the satisfaction we get in taking care of another individual. For many elderly people, the caretaker provides a meaning to life and the motivation to keep going. Having someone care for them and share their concerns helps care-receivers gain a sense of security and place. They feel emotionally comfortable and at home. Together, caregiving and care-taking share a sense of being a dependable bond; this alliance comes only with a kinship whether or not there is mutual affection.

5

Betty Brillo's Diary (Spousal Caregiving)

And yet I have the same feelings as the man who was bitten by the snakes. They say he didn't want to tell anyone what the experience was unless they had been bitten themselves. Since only such a person could understand and forgive him if he ran wild and raved in his agony. And you see I have been bitten by a more painful thing, and in the most painful way that anyone can be bitten in the heart of the soul or whatever else you call it.

—Aleibiddes

Here, Betty, a caretaker, documented and became a witness to her own journey of caring for her husband of 60 years. Her diary illuminates how the challenging and lonely task of caring for a spouse connected her to others. The tipping point in her caregiving happened when she defined herself, at the age of 82, and became her own person. Betty's diary is not a record of unmitigated woe because she was essentially a happy woman. Her genius, as shown in the diary, was how she enjoyed everything offered to her, whether she turned her attention to caregiving, grandchildren, or her dear friends. I chose this diary among many because Betty Brillo was a product of our time, one that left us with what truth there is to tell about spousal caregiving. She made a decision that she would care for her husband and gave it her all. It was not easy for her because she was, in her mind, a very independent woman who always wanted to be free. This diary and other vignettes throughout the book explain how challenging and isolating caregiving can be. They provide different ways of rediscovering and reinventing the complex relationship that develops when people are joined together by illness.

Week 1

My name is Betty Petri Brillo. I am writing this diary because the social worker suggested that it might help other people who are taking care of a sick person. She said writing from the heart during this period might be very therapeutic for me, and that she writes in a journal all the time to help with her own issues in life. Many years ago, my own mother wrote a diary. She destroyed it one day before she took ill. I understand why she destroyed it since I am not sure I would want my only daughter to see how selfish I am regarding the caregiving of my husband of fifty years.

I have been caring for my husband since he retired at age 69, and it has been one illness after another for him. He is losing his eyesight because of diabetes. Last year he had his aortic valve replaced and a pacemaker inserted. Fortunately I've been in good health, and everyone says I'm as strong as an ox.

I married Dom on Thanksgiving Day 50 years ago. I was twenty and Dom was twenty-three. Our family is very close. We have one daughter and two sons, all married and successful. I have five bright little grandchildren who adore me and whom I love more than myself. They cherish Dom. Little Michael told Dom, "I know you can't see very well, Poppy, so I can be your eyes when we play checkers."

After the kids were born, Dom bought me the first washing machine in the neighborhood. He has always treated me well, so I decided to be a good wife and a good mother all my married life. I gave up the dream of owning my own bakery. This was the way it was then. I prayed to God and told him my plan, to stay married my whole life, raise fine educated children, and live to see my grandchildren. But most of all, I never wanted be a burden to anyone. So far, I have been successful.

Even though I have happiness, good health, and all the material things I could ever have wished for, caregiving has changed my life. I'm tired. I want to take care of myself at this point. I take good care of my husband, but there are times when I want to give it all up and get in bed myself. Sometimes I get very confused and upset. Is it possible to get to the point where you just don't want to be a caregiver anymore? I'm sure my mother would call me selfish. Dom is a very good man, and he worked all his life to provide a comfortable life for our children.

Dom and I made a promise many years ago that we would never go to a nursing home. Back then, nursing homes were for people who didn't have children to take good care of them. I decided I would take care of Dom for the rest of his life. It is not easy though, and sometimes I think it consumes my whole life. I know he needs more than the in-home services and care I can provide. It breaks my heart to see him like this.

I told my feelings to the social worker, and she said we could meet to talk once a week in her office, with the family or alone, if I wanted. She set up home care options through the Elder Services. We're entitled to a homemaker once a week and a home health aid three times a week. The price for the services is pretty reasonable, thankfully. Our income enables us to pay for the help on a sliding scale of thirty dollars a month. We aren't entitled to help on weekends, but my children offered to pitch in. I refused. My kids have very busy lives, and I don't want them to have to give up their weekends. A day never goes by that my children do not call and ask us if we need anything. That really helps me feel good, but the best thing is that Dom spends time speaking with them on the telephone. A telephone call means so much to him now. Usually I don't need much from them, except if something breaks in the house, and Dom tries to fix it and makes it worse (like the kitchen faucet. It drips even more now). He was never one for handy things anyway. I am still strong and can handle most things around the house. But I digress. On the weekends, one of my children invites us over for dinner, and we truly appreciate this. Dom doesn't like to go out much anymore. He used to be the man about town and had many friends, but many of them have died—and the others stopped coming by or calling. His eyes are blue and squinty and are not as piercing as they used to be. His voice is still soft even when he is frustrated and angry. He is embarrassed by his disabilities. To tell the truth, sometimes I am too. He holds onto me like a cane and tells me that I'm his eyes now. He is smart and has been a wonderful father and grandfather. But I hate it when he gets frustrated, yells, and curses. At first I took it seriously, but then I realized that I am the only one he can show his anger to. I've stopped trying to rationalize with him at those times. I leave the room, but that doesn't make it any easier.

Dom refused the "meal-on-wheels." He's way too prideful; he's always been. He still is a good cook but makes such a mess that I have to clean every time he cooks anything. Maybe I can do this. Dom is a good man and worked all his life, sometimes two jobs to support us. This much he deserves from me. Dom hasn't been taking his diabetes seriously. I only found out years after his diagnosis that he had it. He was dieting and exercising at that time, so when he was losing all the weight, I thought it was from exercise. When his eyesight started to go and he needed insulin, my whole family got into the act. Everything became more difficult once he retired. He used to have a secretary and people always catering to him. I guess I became his catering staff.

WEEK 2

I took Dom to the eye doctor this morning. If only I had a nickel for every doctor's appointment we went to, I'd have a big chunk of change. Dom also had a reaction from the diabetes and looked pretty out of it. He seemed to perk up after some graham crackers. When he keeps his sugar under control, he's kind and gentle. Once it gets out of control, he is a different person—demanding, frustrated, and unable to see much. The eye doctor suggested cataract surgery and several laser treatments. This would mean two one-hour appointments a week. I am so glad I drive. The big problem, however, is that Dom is always giving me directions and telling me where to go and how to drive. Though he is legally blind, he still has a marvelous sense of direction. When I was sixty years old, my children gave me a series of driving lessons for my birthday. Dom was off the wall when I learned to drive. He didn't believe that women should drive. Dom won't admit it, but I am a good driver. We had a 1970 brown Impala with a shift, no air conditioning, and roll-up windows, and the upholstery perpetually smelled of El Producto cigars that Dom used to light up as soon as he got in the car. I loved and hated that car.

Dom went bananas when he thought he would have to pay for help. He has become very frugal in his old age. He feels strongly that we have to save our money in case something big happens. He remembers what it was like during World War II, with gas rationing and food stamps. The Visiting Nurse Association will send a physical therapist three times a week to help Dom with exercise. His legs are stiff, and he said it's difficult to walk. I urge him to walk in the house or go out to the porch every day, but he's not cooperative. I spend one hour on our exercise bike each day because I believe it helps me stay fit. I can only pray he will listen to the physical therapist.

WEEK 3

Last week was one big headache. First, the Home Care Coordinator spent an hour and a half asking questions and writing in her book. Dom got tired and testy. When she left, he told me to cancel all the help. Then I fought with him about using the exercise bike. He acted like a two-year-old, but he did go on the bike. The Home Health Aid visited us twice this week, and she is jolly, cheerful, and fat. She changed the sheets and cleaned the bathroom. Dom would not allow her to give him a shower. The physical therapist is a young man, and Dom likes him very much. Dom followed every bit of his advice and got on the bike for over fifteen minutes. The visiting nurse comes once a week to check on his pills and oxygen. A woman, who is a Home Health Aid and from Brazil, comes over every day for two hours to set him up for a shower and keeps his room clean. She likes Dom and treats him like a person. The children chipped in, and now we have a cleaning person (her cousin), who comes once a week. Sometimes I think my house is a revolving door. Sometimes I think it makes me work harder.

On Friday, he said I abandoned him by having all these people come to the house to take care of him. I went down to the wine cellar and had a cigarette. Dom never allowed me to smoke, but he knows that I do occasionally.

Dom is waking up during the night to go to the bathroom and always wakes me up to tell me. I know I have to have patience and be courageous, but sometimes I get angry. The social worker told me that my rosary beads are a wonderful relaxation technique. Many days I say them two or three times. For a little bit, I forget all my troubles.

WEEK 4

The insulin comes in measured form now, so all Dom does is give himself the shot. When I am home, he acts as if he cannot do it, but the nurse said he could, so I tell him that he must do it.

On Sunday I drove the Toyota to the eight o'clock mass. I needed to get out of the house, and Dom was still in bed. I laughed when I put the car in drive.

Dom never wanted to get an automatic so I had to learn all these shifts. The breeze felt so nice. The windows in the car were all open, and cool air flew through the car.

I parked in front of the statue of Saint Mary that my sister and brothers had put up in the front yard of the church in my parents' memory. I always look up at it and say, "Hi, Ma. Hi, Pa. Thank you for life." I like coming to this mass since Father Andolfi is a quiet, gentle soul. Though his voice is soft, his sermons always inspire me and give me hope. He is not like that arrogant womanizer Father Naples, who has been giving me the eye for over 30 years. He's a creep.

When I close my eyes here and pray, I'm far away from my responsibilities and life. Don't get me wrong, I have had a wonderful life. Those wall plaques of the Stations of the Cross remind me that Christ carried his cross with dignity and no complaints, and so I have my own cross to bear. Does everyone here have crosses to bear like mine? I don't think so. How quiet it is here. I took my diary to church, is that wrong? Actually, I am writing in it now, God forgive me. Everyone around me looks like they are in a deep trance. I bet they get to live their lives for themselves. Of course everyone calls to inquire how we are doing, but does anyone come over and give me a break? Well, yes, there is Nella. She and I are such good friends, and she never lets me down. She still checks in with me every day and comes over to have lunch with us. St. Mary, please give many blessings to Nella and keep her well. She is over 350 lbs, and I worry about her.

When the organ music starts, everyone around me seems to wake up from a trance. Everyone from the old neighborhood is here today. I miss them still. I went to coffee hour in the basement of the church. Annie, Josie, Tommy, and all my old friends were talking and laughing. I want to laugh too. Everyone asks for Dom and reminds me of what waits for me at home. Lately, when Dom wakes in the morning, he is grouchy and mean-spirited. I try to tell myself that it's the diabetes. I try not to let it bother me, and I bite my tongue.

Mario from the club tapped me on the shoulder to ask about Dom. I said, "He is coming along and puts one foot in front of another every day." Why doesn't Mario go visit him and ask Dom himself? What an ungrateful son of a bitch—after all Dom did for Tommy when he was down and out and almost lost his business. Dom co-signed a loan at the Lawrence Savings Bank, and now Tommy has made it big. Oh, God forgive me, I am swearing in church. I turned my eyes to the statue of St. Rita dressed in a black nun's robe and carrying a rose, and said "God forgive me," but some of these people are not for real.

On the way home I'll stop at the Italian Bakery and buy some bread dough. Today I will make my special fried dough sprinkled with sugar, and my grandchildren will flock over, and I will be happy.

To my pleasant surprise, Nella was sitting with Dom when I came back from church, picking on a blueberry muffin as she listened to him. When we moved to this house on Prospect Hill, I was so depressed because I missed my family and friends, but when I met Nella, it was like a little miracle. I wanted her life, except I wanted to keep my slim figure. She is my best friend, and if it weren't for her, I would be nuts up here with all the German people who live on the hill and aren't friendly to us. I have learned so much from her. She lets everything roll off her back. Her husband is a judge in the Lawrence District Court. I love her because she does not put on any airs, like many of the other women I know who have moved up in society. She lives in the most beautiful house on Prospect Hill and drives a beautiful air-conditioned car. She has two very educated daughters. She is not the best housekeeper and does not like to cook. She always makes Dom laugh, and I am pleased to see the twinkle back in his eye. She is like oxygen for him. I made plans with Nella to go shopping and have lunch tomorrow.

Week 5

I have decided to get some help on the weekends so that I do not have to worry about rushing and having a stroke like the one my father did when he was sixty-three years old. That would be all I need. The homemaker will be here in five minutes, so I feel comfortable about taking a walk. Dom likes her, and since her name is Maria, like his mother, he is very cooperative. She is Brazilian and lives in our old neighborhood. Best of all, she likes Dom and treats him with respect. Dom allows her to give him a shave, and she offered to cut his hair next week. She has permission to work for us for four hours on the weekends. My children pay her twelve dollars an hour. I don't feel bad about this because I keep a record of the money, and when we sell our house, I will pay them back. I made the decision that I didn't have to hang around when the helpers came. I stopped treating them as if they were company, cleaning, baking cookies for them, and making the house smell nice. I used to feel guilty . . . sometimes I still do, but not today. I realize I am a better person when I get some time off. I went to the corner store and bought Dom a lottery ticket—each number for a grandchild's birthday, as always. The ticket is something for Dom to do, and he keeps busy watching TV to get the numbers. I am remembering how years ago it was illegal to gamble. My cousin John was a bookie, and once when he was caught, he almost went to jail. My brothers were furious, but Dom never condemned him. Now everyone can gamble. How things change. I too have changed, but now I am thinking how happy we were with the kids when they were little. It's different now. I think it's because I kept changing all my life, and Dom is still the same man I married.

Week 6

Today, before Nella picked me up to go shopping, Dom began complaining that I go out too much. He wanted me to be home when the physical therapist came at 11:45 A.M. It's not the first time he's pulled something like this when I have plans. This time, I called the agency to check on the appointment time, and the appointment with the therapist is really tomorrow. I must double-check all appointments. I made sure to prepare lunch for him—his favorite escarole and white kidney beans with fresh Italian Bread. All he needs to do is heat up the food in the microwave for lunch. My daughter will call him from work to talk with him and remind him to eat.

We stopped at Morin's Bakery before going shopping. Nella needed a dress to go to a banquet with her husband, so we went to Russems. She bought three dresses, rhinestone earrings, necklace, and a pearl bracelet. Nella told me to buy something special for myself. I didn't really have a use for a pretty dress, but I could not resist a navy crepe dress with a beautiful white gardenia print, and to top it all off some pearl earrings. Gardenias are my favorite flower. Mrs. Russem, the store-owner's wife, came over and said I could take the dress on credit and pay for it weekly. I love beautiful clothes, and I take good care of them so they will be ready to wear if I go to a funeral or wedding. At my age there always seems to be one or the other. The older I get, it seems more of the former. We walked three blocks to Kap's men's store. Nella wanted to take the car, but I said the walk would do us good. We could digest that big lunch. Nella purchased five shirts, two ties, a dozen monogrammed handkerchiefs, and a leather belt for her husband. Dom used to dress better before he retired and got sick. I argue with him at times because I want him to look nice when helpers come to the house or when we go to the kids' homes on Sunday. I purchased two cotton short-sleeved sport shirts, 3 white undershirts, and a pair of tan socks. Old Mr. Kapelson came over to say hello and ask about Dom. They were good friends and played cards together years ago. He is still a friend and calls Dom right on schedule once every two weeks. My god, where are the people Dom did favors for, I think to myself. As we were leaving, he gave me six beautiful white cotton handkerchiefs and said, "Tell Dom I am thinking about him. You've got a good man there, Betsy." I was about to cry but kept my chin up and thanked him.

When we got home, Dom was making his famous tomato sauce and fried eggplants. He gave Nella two bottles of the sauce and a plate of eggplant. She asked for his recipe, and for a minute, you could see the spring back in his step. Of course I know she will never make them. The kitchen was a disaster with all the cooking and frying. She didn't seem to notice.

Later That Week

What a morning this was. I was walking to the mailbox, and a scream came from the house. "Betty, Betty!" I dropped the mail, ran up the stairs, and found Dom on the phone with his heart monitor, calling in for his monthly check for his pacemaker. The beeping was loud, and he was very upset. "Something is

Dom's Fried Eggplant

- Slice the eggplant with a meat slicer (my brother gave us one from the store).
- Lay the slices in a huge colander.
- Salt each layer and then cover with a dish.
- Add a large can of tomatoes on the dish as a weight.
- Drain for at least 2 hours (all the bitterness goes out of the eggplant as liquid). Be sure to wash all the salt from the eggplant slices.
- Put 3 eggs in a soup plate and add a dash of salt and a bit of water, and mix with a fork.
- Lay out a piece of waxed paper and put 1 cup of bread flour, some chopped parsley, grated parmigiano cheese, and a good dash of kosher salt. Mix well.
- Heat a medium amount of Filipo Berrio Olive Oil in a large frying pan.
- Lay out some paper towels on the counter.
- Dip the drained eggplant in the egg wash and then in the flour mixture.
- Fry quickly and gently turn over. Lay each slice on paper towels to drain oil.
- Put in a bake-proof casserole dish the layers of cooked eggplant, cover with thin slice of cheese and tomato sauce, and continue this way until all three are used up. Cover the top with grated Parmesan cheese and sprinkle oil over the top.
- Cover with aluminum foil and bake at 350° for 20 minutes.
- Eggplant can be served hot and is good cold. (You can bake rather than fry the eggplant; it's healthier, but not the way we make it in my house.)

wrong with my pacemaker," he said. The nurse on the other end of the phone said, "Take it easy; there is nothing wrong with your pacemaker." She asked if he was near a microwave, and he was (making water for tea). Everything turned out fine, although my blood pressure must have risen 10 points, and my letters were scattered all over the street.

Dom's anxiety is wearing me down. Lately I've been trying to go back to some of my hobbies. I like to make knitted hats and gloves for the grandkids. Last year I made 100 hats and they sold them at the church fair.

Week 7

Dom had an off week. His friend Bud called him from the Bon Secour Hospital. Bud began dialysis treatments because of kidney failure. Like Dom, Bud also has diabetes. Dom came into the kitchen later and said Bud was sick, and then Dom had a diabetic reaction. I gave him some orange juice, and that seemed to calm him down. He didn't want to talk about Bud or why his blood sugar was so low. We have been through this many times, but his sugar fluctuations are always very scary and upsetting for both of us. I'll stay with him the rest of the day. We sat in the den for a while and looked at some old photograph albums. He said he thinks he is going to die. He was fine after a few hours and back to watching *The Price Is Right*. This was a tough week. Tony, our son, came over afterwards and had his daughter Kimberly with him.

Dom was himself again. Oh how he loves seeing his grandchildren. They are the light of his life. You would never guess how different he was compared to this morning.

Week 8

I am writing while I sit in the Emergency Room at Lawrence General Hospital. It is nine days before Christmas, and the place is buzzing. I feel comfortable here even though I am crying. I am physically alone, but not alone emotionally. No one can see my tears because I am wearing sunglasses. The Triage Nurse who interviewed me said that I might be here a while because the other patients have more serious injuries. I look just fine, but I fell hard on the ice outside my house and drove myself here. She said I could possibly have a concussion, but couldn't be sure until I was evaluated. Everyone here seems to be bleeding. A 10-year-old freckle-faced boy is holding a dishcloth to cover his eye. His father is gently holding the boy's head to his own shoulder. His father says to me, "He's a brave kid . . . this is routine for him." Mrs. Cohen is sitting in a wheelchair talking to Mrs. Calaveri about Christmas and Hannuka. The two holidays fall close together this year. The talk turns to food and cooking, and the conversation becomes animated. Mrs. Cohen is 90 years old and still makes latkes, and Mrs. Calaveri is going on and on about her cheesecake. Mr. Calaveri and Mrs. Cohen's sons are watching the holiday cooking show on TV. I hope I get home so I can make that Italian cheesecake for Christmas. A well-dressed man and his wife come into the emergency room, his nose scraped, and he's holding a washcloth to it covered in blood. He is dressed in a suit, and his shoes shine like patent leather. She is much younger than he is and laughing and then complaining, "There is going to be a long wait." She rubs me the wrong way.

I had to leave the house this morning. Dom was criticizing me about sticky counters and not sending out the Christmas cards this year. He was distressed because he hit his thumb with a hammer trying to put up one of those many pictures in the den. He keeps changing them around for something to do. Mostly, he changes the boys around. Once, when Dom Jr. did not call for two weeks, he turned his picture facing the wall. Dom was angry because of his injury and started cussing. I don't like this kind of behavior during the holidays, or really any day. It was a sign for me to get out of his way, so I put my sneakers on and took a walk. I thought I would go to the jewelry store downtown. I wanted to buy for Lisa, my namesake granddaughter, a pair of pearl earrings for Christmas. Actually, I had already purchased her gifts, and they were all wrapped. I purchased and wrapped forty-five gifts this year in order to be sure I had enough presents for everyone. Who knows if I'll be around next year. This way, they will have something to remember me by. Anyway, as I ran outside, I slipped on some black ice. I hit my head and tailbone. A very nice Asian man stopped his green truck and helped me up. As I got up, I told myself I had to be more careful. As I did, I slipped again and hurt myself in the same place. This time a woman stopped her Chevy in front of the snow bank and picked me up. I told her I was fine, and she left. I went into the house because I was aching pretty badly. I told Dom I was going to the hospital just to check things out. I asked him not to tell the kids if they called. He was concerned, but otherwise okay, so I drove myself to the hospital.

The man with the black shiny shoes said he also fell on the ice while trying to open a frozen lock on the car's passenger-side door. I thought about how nice he was to be opening the door for his wife. I miss that. His wife was still complaining about the wait. Now I am remembering that when I fell, I didn't want to go back to my house. Even now I would like to stay in this emergency room where someone will take care of me. The triage nurse brought out some ice packs for several of us. The wife of the man with the black shiny shoes laughed nervously and said, "Now we won't be seen for hours." I am lucky because I had my little diary in my pocketbook, and I can observe and write. Whenever I tell Dom I will be going out for a minute, an hour, or an afternoon, he distracts me by asking for something, and then I forget either what I'm writing or what I'm supposed to do.

A woman wearing an argyle sweater and beautiful leather brown boots just brought her teenage son in the emergency room. She asks me if I have been waiting long. I tell her about 1/2 hour, and then my phone rang. I missed a call. The overworked RN called me over to take my vital signs and fill out more papers. She explained I would probably be in the emergency room for at least four hours. She thought I could wait since I can drive and others could not. I told her that I had a very sick husband and asked if she could see me as early as possible. I guess if someone had to drive me here she would see me earlier. She felt sorry for me and tried her best.

After my x-rays were over, and nothing was broken, the doctor said I could go home. I heard someone calling "Mom." It was my daughter Joanne. She left work when I did not answer the cell phone she had given me for Christmas. I was relieved to see someone I loved.

Week 9

Dom is feeling better about himself and his accomplishments. He does not need the walker or cane and takes care of his own toileting. His friends Chuck and Tommy came over to see him, and I served lunch. Dom was in such a good mood when they left, it was like he was back to his old self again. I never knew he helped them when they had money problems and co-signed a loan for them at the bank. They paid him back and have never forgotten his kind deed, and that led us into a discussion about our life together. I learned so many things about Dom that I never knew before. I feel this is a turning point in my caretaking.

Week 10

I have a double hernia that my doctor found after I complained of a lump in my belly. It's especially upsetting because I won't be able to care for Dom.

This is not an easy thing to accept, because I cannot be ill at a time like this. Dr. Choo sent me to a surgeon who confirmed the diagnosis. He said I could wait a while to get it fixed, but I should really have it done before I get too old. I have myself to blame since I have been lifting heavy things all of my life. The clay pots I move around the yard were heavy, and the bags of groceries were heavy. Dom said I should have it done as soon as possible. The risk is that the hernia could strangulate and cause much more harm. The surgeon said that I could have a weakness from genetics and the births of so many children.

Week 11

Caregiving is much harder now that I can't lift anything. The stairs even seem like an insurmountable task. It makes me worried—who will care for Dom? I called the local grocery store to have our groceries delivered. It became a problem when they said the only way to get a delivery is by using the Internet. I spoke to the manager about this because since I have no expertise on the computer, it would be difficult for me. My daughter eventually came over and set me up. People who do not have computers are unable to do this. I hope my complaint to the store manager will be taken seriously. When the delivery boy brought the groceries into the kitchen, I was so surprised how many bags I have been carrying all my life.

Betty Brillo's husband, Dom, died two years after her first diary entry. In all the time I knew her, her main concern was "not to interrupt her children's lives with her problems." She used every means available to "keep my promise at the alter of marriage." After the appropriate mourning period, she sold her home where she lived for over 60 years. She sat on her front porch while her children and grandchildren ran a huge yard sale. One man wanted to buy one of Dom's Stetson hats and she told him to take the "whole bunch" of them for two dollars. She entered an assisted living facility where she became the sage advisor to many of the residents. She joined the singing group, the cooking group, the reading group, and often led the exercise group. She died peacefully surrounded by her children and grandchildren.

6

THE STORY OF ILLNESS

Illness arrives, literally out of nowhere. Newly ill, the patient immediately recalls the sick days of childhood . . . As an adult illness makes him feel out of place, unaccountably absent far outside existence.

—Michael Stein, *The Lonely Patient*

Illness has great meaning and affects people's social relationships, self-image, and behaviors. Illness is what the patients and families bring to the doctor. Some take longer to run their course, and the illnesses that affect our elderly parent, spouses, and loved ones often never entirely disappear. This chapter is concerned with those chronic illnesses that never entirely disappear. In addition, these chronic illnesses in old age vary greatly, but they have two things in common for the sick person and family: feelings of "Why me?" and "What can be done?" Disease is different because it is what the physician has been trained to identify through an interview, physical examinations, and medical tests. Illness has a very private significance for the patient. For many it means the loss of confidence in one's health, betrayal, terror, loneliness, and loss. The varieties of chronic illness are many, and some of the frail and elderly have several chronic illnesses. The chronically ill are our parents, grandparents, siblings, aunts, uncles, friends, and coworkers.

To understand how illness is interpreted by elderly loved ones, listen to their stories. Storytelling is nourishment and helps an aging parent talk about life's high points and low points. What is even more important, however, is for the caregiver to be a witness to this life story and for the care-receiver have an opportunity to reaffirm the bond with the survivors who will carry on the tale once the person is dead. One of my finest roles as a social worker was to listen to the narrative of a frail elderly patient who had no one to tell his story to. There are fewer truer tragedies at life's end.

The caregiver is brought into a fearful world of pain, disability, and suffering. The patient and the family share the equally the uncertain world of the pain and vulnerability. In the old days people who died from chronic illnesses got them quickly, the crisis came quickly, and one either died or pulled through. Today, most illnesses in old age are chronic and slow-acting and can be treated and not cured. Each chronic illness brings with it multiple problems, including role changes, marriage disruption, loss of mobility, and stigmatization. Some days, when things go bad, patients feels awful and wish the crisis or illness would go away; some wish they were dead. On good days, when they are feeling better they forgets their suffering and display a happy, joyous disposition. Oliver Sacks calls these times "personal moments, life-moments, crucial moments" (Stein 11) while death is always on someone's mind. Many times a patient develops a new self as his old identity is taken away from him. There is so much that is lost during a siege of illness, and the caregiver is often unable to restore what is lost. A committed caretaker cannot pull away from when the life of the patient revolves around the events of crisis and symptoms. When the illness gets out of control, it has the power to influence everyone in the kin network. The patient, despite his disease, wants to live a normal life.

Mr. R. was a 72-year-old widower when he began treatment as a result of Parkinson's disease. When I met him, he was working three days a week in a law firm, and on the surface, he seemed well put together in spite of his Parkinson's. His family dynamics were multilayered, and he did not feel that it was important for his family to know about his diagnosis in spite of the fact that it was hereditary. During the time I knew him, he was intensely occupied with "living a normal life" and keeping his diagnosis a secret from family and colleagues. As Michael Stein (2007) wrote, "health is familiar, predictable, reliable, and we hope enduring. It provides a sense of orientation. Illness is a break in the established, continuous sameness and comfort of health. Betrayal arrives without arrangement, unpredictably, spontaneously carrying danger."

His favorite person was Franklin D. Roosevelt, and like Mr. Enrico he knew everything about Roosevelt. His greatest fear was that he would interrupt his children's lives, so he made me promise not to interrupt his children's lives by contacting them about his disease.

His admission to the hospital changed everything. He hated that an ambulance brought him to the hospital. I encouraged him to let his children know because they must have been worried about him. Eventually his doctor convinced him, and his doctor was the one who called his oldest son. His oldest son called everyone else. I met his family for the first time in the hospital; they were a positive, loving, caring family—faced with an abrupt transformation of their father from his appearing totally well to lying in a hospital bed. He was pale, with tubes running from him, and unable to care for himself—this was a shock to him.

Mr. R. kept his loneliness to himself until he was admitted to the hospital. "Illness induces and perhaps demands loneliness. One is lonely because there is nothing to be done to alter this state. The part and quality and intensity of the loneliness of illness depend on the patient's attachment to his body and what he needs it for" (Stein 176). Before his crisis, Mr. R. depended and trusted that his body would not betray him. When he became sick, his stoicism was not available to him. He felt unprotected. He began to recede into depression and was referred to a psychiatrist for treatment.

Most hospital patients feel joyous when family members arrive at the hospital to visit. On the day his family visited him, he did not open his eyes. I met with the family in his room, and he eventually became talkative. Was he in a state of terror or a state of loss and surrender? It is hard to know. What I do know is that Mr. R. spent so much time keeping his secret from his family that now that they knew and were there to help him, he felt relieved. So were his caretakers. "I'm OK and will be just fine," Mr. R. said, waving to everyone in the room as they left.

Because the control of symptoms is linked with adherence to regimens, as in the case of a diabetic who is insulin-dependent, there is always a constant threat or crisis. Without insulin, the diabetic may fall into insulin coma and die; the epileptic can go into a convulsion and be killed in a fall or a traffic accident. We feel helpless when we cannot control events. In order to not feel helpless, caregivers and possibly their family must always be organized to handle all contingencies. Helplessness adds to feelings of confusion and incompetent decision making. The lifestyle and social relationships that people have been accustomed to may call for major adjustments. A person who was outgoing, gregarious, vibrant, and full of confidence prior to illness may feel betrayed by his body. "Health is familiar, predictable, reliable and we hope enduring . . . The patient has trusted his body up to that point and taken good care of it. Why has it turned on him? This sense of betrayal is too enormous to manage—it swamps the patient, causing him to feel useless" (Stein 61). A person who has a chronic illness plus pain is physically isolated from the mainstream of life. Sometimes the caregiver gets impatient. But she also is thinking about her own genes and her parents' histories and what she has inherited. Friends and relatives may withdraw from people who make excessive demands, and often even physicians advise spouses or family quite literally to abandon the sick person: "It's time to put him in a nursing home." It makes no sense. "It's better for her," they say. And because the sick person is aware of having become an intolerable burden, she may accept those rationales and report that those professionals treating her "know best." The person becomes lonely in her body's betrayal.

According to Oliver Sacks, as soon as the person crosses into the land of sickness, she is in "No-land, Nowhere . . . fallen off the map, the world of the knowable" (Stein 17). Often this journey to this "No-land" and the first sign of the body's betrayal is pain. None of us like pain; in fact, we hate pain. Some people keep pain diaries and track the severity of pain. Joe Tenses was a person who kept such a diary. He tracked his pain for 12 and sometime 20 hours a day. He could not think of anything else. He attended a pain clinic and said that did not help. Deeply disappointed, he felt that his body had betrayed him. In the hospital he asked for more and more pain medication. His wife told me he had a stash of pain medications at home. As a last resort, he consented to surgery that would sever a nerve so that he would not feel any pain. He became wheelchair-bound. As his sense of body betrayal grew, he became critical of his wife and children. Joe felt that his body had betrayed him, and he came to hate it. His family, however, felt the worst betrayal because they could not help him.

There are no formulas, no prototypes on how to be sick or how to grow old. Perhaps there are no answers to all the extraordinary questions about illness, growing old, or caretaking. But as I listened to the thousands of stories of people who were ill I realized that in someway they evoked all our stories. I kept hearing in my head,—perhaps the voices of ancestors—saying, "people are resilient and adaptable, and through their struggles a new, creative path will make its way." Once I became more vulnerable myself, I was better able to personalize my own life. Not as a social worker, mother, sister, aunt, or grandmother but as a person facing aging herself, sometimes fearfully, wondering what the future will bring. Always thanking God that I am living in a century where we can choose our life roles and paths. We can study the ongoing life, but only by listening to people's stories and doing something for them—and with them—can we activate in the person who is ill all the strength in her historical development and record for them their place in history. Once we open those doors and when we really listen to the experience of other people we become more vulnerable ourselves. We also take part in the healing as caretakers while we heal ourselves, and so many doors will open.

7

MOTHERS AND DAUGHTERS

By taking care of my mother, I came to understand how much I loved her, and how much she loved me. And this made it all the more moving when she was able to take her old role back. When I told her during a telephone conversation that I had a sore throat and she said, "I wish I was there to make you some tea," it was as if she did make me tea.

—Deborah Tannen, *You're Wearing That?*

Getting old is not easy, and when physical and cognitive deficits make caregiving essential, the first question is, who is available to help? Mothers, if they have daughters, usually turn to those daughters. If they do not have a daughter, a son or daughter-in-law or other relative often assumes the caregiving role. But the caregiving relationship between mothers and daughters has unique challenges and rewards. These relationships are especially complex for all women because the struggle to find a balance between letting go and achieving independence has been with them all their lives.

In writing about aging daughters and elderly mothers, I do not mean to negate the great contribution made to caregiving by sons, husbands, and grandfathers. But experts who have never been women cannot tell the true caregiving stories recounted by women. A decade ago, Betty Brillo wrote in her diary the truth about spousal caretaking—because she could never speak about it publicly without fear that everyone, including her daughters who loved her and whom she loved more than anything in the world, would suspect lack of devotion to her husband. Of the hundreds of women I have counseled, many have had similar stories and feelings.

There are few relationships as complex as the relationship between mother and daughter. The relationship is often characterized by both love and strength and by pain and stress. The relationship with the same-sex parent is pivotal for emotional health, and the mother–daughter relationship shapes the child in unique ways. For a daughter who has been her mother's apprentice since birth, watching her mother's every move will lead to learning both good and bad habits and notions. Daughters learn to model their mother's behavior, choosing to follow their mother's lead or rejecting that lead. For many women, being a mother as well as having a mother is profound. A strong mother–daughter relationship in later life invokes a balance of positive and negative feelings for many reasons, the primary one being that they share an experience as women. Relative to all other ties during an illness, mother-and-daughter ties can be the closest both emotionally and psychologically. In young adulthood the relationship may be an idealized interconnectedness, and the need for the daughter to become financially, psychologically, and physically independent creates a climate of unintentional struggle. In later life, aging daughters and elderly mothers can frustrate each other. Because an elderly mother has known her daughter all her life, she may think she has exclusive rights to tell her "the truth as it is" or that she knows best. For example, if someone's mother told her something during childhood that she was angry about her whole life, and that led to the child not trusting herself, the anger from that interpretation by the daughter could interfere with other relationships. Your mother may still know how to criticize, but she is not the same mother now that she is in old age.

When an adult daughter becomes her mother's caregiver, the result is usually an emotional crisis. The daughter must leave behind the rebellion and emancipation of adolescence and early adulthood and, in effect, become a parent to the parent, a role that requires the maturity to let go of past conflicts that may have characterized the relationship. In every respect, the traditional mother–daughter relationship gets turned on its head.

Despite the affinity they may feel for one another, they may also have different perspectives and expectations about caregiving. For the daughter, caregiving may be a necessary but unwelcome burden added to existing family and career demands. For the mother, it may mean accepting, but resenting, her dependency. Though not all ties between adult daughters and aging mothers are the same, as a result of ethnicity, economics, or psychological and social structures, they do have one thing in common: they are the source for each other of great strength, hope, and often emotional pain or stress. Although mothers and daughters feel a strong affinity for each other, they may possess different perspectives about self-care and about giving and accepting advice. The attachment and connection between mothers and daughters become more complex as the mother ages and her health gives way. The roles of middle-age daughters and mothers are not as crystal clear as when the daughter was a child.

Not all mother–daughter relationships are supportive or collaborative in caregiving; the relationship can be one of physical, mental, and emotional inequality. This is not much different from when the daughter was a small child. Despite the new challenges mother and daughter face in this newly redefined relationship, however, for many women caregivers this is an opportunity to repay a debt. At the center of the caregiving relationship in adulthood and old age, there can be a be a sense of reciprocity in which the daughter gives back what was given to her in childhood. Truth-telling between generations is advantageous because when truth-telling is at the center of the relationship, inequality that existed in childhood cannot continue. A daughter can initiate an honorable relationship by trying to be truthful instead of trying to make the mother happy and fill her up with good intentions.

The story of Ann, a former client of mine, is instructive. When Ann was 60, she became the primary caregiver for her widowed 84-year-old mother after her mother suffered a mild heart attack. Ann worked full-time and lived with her husband. Ann's sister Lena, 40, was Ann's only sibling. Lena worked full-time and was recently divorced with three small children. She visited her mother once a week on Saturdays and often took her out to lunch. Both women had positive relationships with their aging widowed mother. The situation changed when Lena's marriage fell apart before her mother became ill. During this time Lena accepted not only emotional support from her mother but financial support as well. When her mother became ill, Lena was working full-time and had custody of her children.

The sisters, because of their age difference, never had a relationship with one another that was as close as the relationship each had with their mother. In the beginning, it was assumed that Ann would do the "lion's share" of the caretaking because she was the oldest, and her children were grown. As their mother became more dependent, conflicts and struggles between the three women ensued. When I met them, they had been off-and-on caregiving for five years. Ann's husband had since retired and was home all day. Lena had been in a very serious relationship for one year. Neither the mother nor the daughters could clarify what they expected or needed from each other. It appeared as if Ann and Lena were trying to give no more care than was needed to maintain their mother's independence. Yet Ann was "just plain tired" as the demands at work increased, and her husband was "wanting something to do all the time" now that he was not working. She expressed anger that she "could never satisfy" her mother. She was finding that the persistent phone calls from her mother at work were stressful and fatiguing. Her mother in turn experienced aggravation when her daughter was not available. She would make comments such as, "Did you use caller ID and not pick up the phone when I called?" Lena was stopping in on her mother three times a week because she felt "obligated," and occasionally she would bring lunch, which her mother would always find fault with, saying "too much salt" or "I don't eat wraps" and so on.

Their mother, on the other hand, could not mention any specific things her daughters did that caused her to be unhappy. Instead she became critical of the way her daughters managed their own lives. She did not think there were any problems in her relationships with her children. Researchers have found that older mothers of adult daughters, during caregiving, report little conflict when asked about the relationship. This may be because a mother is upset with her daughter without telling her. Many feel that their daughters can never do enough, and they often do not communicate directly with their daughters.

This was the case with Ann, Lena, and their mother. Many of the frustrations between the three women resulted from not talking and not asking each other questions. When Ann's mother criticized her for not answering her telephone calls at work, Ann said nothing to her mother. An explanation, it turned out, as simple as telling her mother that calls were restricted at work could have resolved the anger that set them both up for distress and pent-up emotions. Ann's mother was hurt and disappointed that her daughters did not make time to help her with decisions that she felt she could not make alone. Yet she never asked them. The two daughters started responding differently to their mother, which was clearly not an easy task. Ann shared with her mother the worries she had about Lena, who was living alone with two small children. Ann began asking her mother for advice on how her mother handled her father's retirement. Lena missed her mother's support, both financial and emotional, and began reciprocating. She located the new apartment for her mother where supports were available, helped pick out the furniture, and visited until her mother was comfortable in her new surroundings. The mother, uncomfortable at first about telling her daughters how she really felt, did make some changes. She told her daughters of the loneliness she felt living alone. The mother stopped pitting one daughter against the other and stopped criticizing her daughters' choices. Small changes, but if the situation had continued on a downward spiral, three women would have fallen into a void. And as their mother became sicker, they were able to provide what she needed at the end of life. The mother, on the other hand, was so happy that the daughters finally "had each other."

Daughters in caregiving situations tend to feel a combination of burden and enrichment. Because this emotional bond is so important to both the mother and the daughter, it can be an added stress for the daughter. If the daughter and mother work through conflicts and respect each other's differences, the relationship will be one of reciprocity. The concept of reciprocity in caregiving and care-receiving, I believe, is invaluable. It provides a useful model for other close relationships. If the conflicts cannot be worked out, the actual caregiving relationship can continue, but it will not be as rewarding. The caregiving relationship between mothers and daughters is likely to mirror that of childhood. Now, however, the daughter is attending to her mother, and thus, the intense process may cause exaggerated emotions, some still unhealed from childhood. The mother should respond in kind by respectfully understanding her daughter's needs.

Caregiving can be a mending, important, and sometimes spiritual experience for both aging daughter and mother on a number of levels. Though not all mother–daughter relationships are supportive at the time of a parent's illness, they can be become so if the parties focus on the task at hand, in helping the ill parent navigate an illness. Emotional ties at middle and later life are enduring. It is important for adult daughters to preserve the roles they have shared all their lives. If the daughter becomes the mother, she denies her own lifelong role of child throughout adulthood. Swapping roles and becoming a mother to your own mother is a pathological role reversal. It is important to remember that even if your mother is physically and mentally incapacitated, she is still your mother. This tie is part of an inherited behavior in humans.

The daughter who becomes a caregiver at the time of her mother's decline or illness is in essence taking the overall responsibility of another life. It is unlike taking care of a baby, however, where most new mothers coalesce and find themselves growing in many ways. Instead, a daughter's caregiving can last for the remainder of her mother's life. A working daughter may have to cut down her work hours or hire additional help to support her mother. A retired daughter may not have the endurance for what is required. Many elderly women live alone and have established independent lives. Many older women who were very independent reported to me that they did not want to burden their children, but if necessary their choice for a caretaker would be their daughter.

The story of Mrs. Kiernan illustrates how an independent care-receiver and her adult daughter maintain a good caregiving relationship. Mrs. Kiernan is an elderly widowed woman who insists on living in her own small house by herself. She insists she is "not old," and even further, she "does not feel old." She has a written statement by her lawyer stating that she would refuse to go to a nursing home. She accepts little help from her daughter Pam, causing Pam to worry that she might find her injured on the floor someday. Mrs. Kiernan does not deny she is at risk but wants to retain her privacy and independence. Her daughter solved the problem by getting the lifeline (emergency alert watch or necklace) that Mrs. Kiernan is now happy wearing as her new watch, and Pam calls her mother frequently. She provided her mother with a cell phone that her mother finds useful. Pam has done what she can while still maintaining her mother's independence. When her daughter visits her, Mrs. Kiernan reports they have a "good time" exchanging old recipes and revisiting old photographs of the happy times at the seashore.

Pam told me that if her mother did not know where she was and could not live on her own anymore, she would consider an alternate to her current living situation. Pam said that worrying provoked her to interfere with her mother's care, and when that happened, she knew her mother had a long list of direct attacks that would evoke feelings of guilt. It then would become a war that neither of them could win. Pam acknowledged that she knew her mother's flaws and was willing to transcend them during the caregiving relationship.

Pam respected her mother's wishes for independence and autonomy, giving her mother no more care than she already needed. Her mother refused help from "strangers" in the beginning but realized that the reciprocal relationship with outside help required trust and responsiveness, and in this way the problem was handled positively. It is easy to forget that an aging mother's dignity is at stake when she needs more assistance. Part of a daughter's caregiving responsibility and privilege is to assure her mother that she has self-worth by respecting her mother's wishes. Mothers can make their preferences known by telling their daughters what they want and by asserting themselves.

The theme of wanting to be separate and yet close in this relationship is common to many mother–daughter pairs. Mrs. Kiernan was exceptional to some degree because she valued her independence and made clear what her wishes were before she became ill. She also tried really hard to understand her daughter's constraints by understanding her point of view.

Oftentimes, elderly mothers do not ask for what they want or what they need because they think that this will be asking their daughters for more than what they can give. Instead the mother says, "She never has time for me. I don't know her private life; she only tells me things that she thinks make me happy or things that criticize my appearance." Adult daughters can give suggestions and coach their mothers by keeping them updated on current events like politics and by sharing details of their lives. Mothers feel that daughters withhold information about themselves even though it is not intentional. Criticism from daughters contributes to the mother feeling low self-esteem and incompetence. Just as negative feelings can occur from conversations, positive feelings can be enhanced by these same conversations by changing the way things are said and adjusting tone of voice and facial expressions.

We all need to feel competent and have a sense that we have some worth. Small acts of caring let other people know that they are cared for. Feelings of self-worth and human dignity can travel silently from one person to another through simple acts of touch. Touch can be a soothing sensation for both caregiver and care-receiver. A daughter reveals her compassionate self while the mother gets a wonderful feeling that she is loved and prized. Many aging mothers are hardly ever touched, except by a nurse or a grandchild. Small examples of caring can mean much more to an aging person than we ever would have realized.

On top of the unpleasant physical manifestations from being elderly or ill, there is a heavy psychological toll as well. Many elderly mothers worry more about losing their independence than about dying. They fear abandonment and becoming useless and helpless. Many daughters go to extreme lengths to preserve their mother's independence; however, their efforts might come into conflict with the need to balance their obligations and competing responsibilities.

Caregiving between mothers and daughters is similar to an enduring marital relationship. In a good caregiving relationship, the two partners influence each other during a time of decision making, stating their points of view openly and always attempting compromise. For example, Lisa shares her mother Ann's good looks and inquisitive blue eyes. Both women share the same tastes in decorating and clothes. When Lisa turned 40, she was a mirror image of her mother; she had married at age 20 and dropped out of college to raise her children until they were grown, and her mother was her best friend. Once Lisa's children were in school, the similarities ended. Lisa went back to school, earning a degree in education, and began working as a teacher. Her mother Ann still cooked up home meals from scratch and picked up Lisa's children from school. She brought them to piano lessons, soccer games, and doctor's appointments. She cared for her husband and home. Lisa, on the other hand, went to the gym every other day before work, served meals that are easy, had a cleaning woman once a week, and had a manicure once a week. Their life choices now could not be any different.

Lisa, who is now 60 years old, has changed, and her mother, who is now 80 years old and who did not have the same opportunities as her daughter, has not changed. Both women have made sacrifices, but given the differences in these sacrifices, can they really understand each other? Lisa's new awareness of her mother's aging brings her face-to-face with her own aging. Furthermore, this awareness can be a positive step in understanding her aging mother.

The daughters of the baby boomer generation have the opportunity for living differently from their mothers. There seems to be a driving force for daughters to be different from their mothers for most of their lives, and daughters have created many ways of affirming their separateness and independence. When your mother is in her seventies, and you are in your fifties, a new awareness arises, and it is impossible to stifle this awareness of aging and death. Daughters fear getting older and looking "like her," and aging mothers fear losing independence and being abandoned.

Good-Enough Daughter

Even if your mother was not a good mother, you can be a "good-enough daughter" who does her best in the caregiving relationship. If you have never been a responsible daughter in your life, here is your chance to make yourself feel good. Once you begin giving all you can to her caregiving, your mother may want more, and you may want to set clear boundaries by discussing what you can reasonably do. It is very difficult to be a responsible daughter during this time, but many people keep trying—and have found that they can provide some companionship and even love. Being a responsible daughter is a good remedy for any guilt.

If your mother never told you she loved you and constantly yelled and was critical, you may feel strongly that she did not take care of you. It is no surprise then that you may not be prepared for this stage in your life. Many people refer to this time as a developmental stage. I call this development stage "Caregiving." In this new development stage, we have the opportunity to create a new paradigm. This new paradigm creates the opportunity for a daughter (whether she had a "good mother," a "good-enough mother," or a terrible mother) to experience growth. It is an opportunity to reverse the childhood dramas that were extremely hurtful. This stage requires planning prior to a mother becoming ill.

Making caregiving a priority for the daughter is not something that happens automatically. If your mom was not a good mother, you may not want to put time, effort, and love into caregiving for her. Caregiving can be an opportunity to mend any cracks in the relationship. You are going above and beyond your duties, especially if you felt uncared for or unappreciated by your mother. Extending yourself, especially in this kind of situation, can cause a variety of emotions. Your knees might shake, and you might pray, but there is no preparation for either party for unexpected circumstances that arise. By not caretaking, you may be closing off a part of you, the part of you that is compassionate.

LIFE REVIEW

Parents who are old are easily engaged in talking about their lives. It is fortunate to be able to review your parents' lives with them; some people wish after their parents' death that they had known more about their parents' early lives. Some old feelings from your childhood that you had totally forgotten about may come up, and these may interfere with caregiving. Recognizing that they are from the past can lessen some anxiety.

One of the best ways to learn about your mother (or father) is to ask what she did before she became your mom, and what were her dreams? What was her favorite memory of childhood? Not only is it an oral history that will benefit your mother, but grandchildren will be intrigued too, and you never know, it may guide them in their future. When a voice or video recorder comes out, it is amazing how your mother is transformed into a young woman again. Reviewing past experiences is a great exercise for the brain, and parents and elderly people get much pleasure from telling their stories.

MOTHERS FEELING USELESS

Many elderly mothers worry more about losing their independence than about dying. They are fearful of becoming useless and helpless. As mothers age, they may take longer to get dressed, may tend to misplace items, and may need to surrender their driver's license. For example, Alice turned 85 this year. She was the primary driver for all her girlfriends to book clubs, lunches, and Canasta games, and she took care of her own home and husband. When she was told that she could not drive any longer and had to give up her license because of macular degeneration, Alice made a decision to stay active. Her daughter and granddaughter taught her how to use the computer and the magnifying machine that was provided by the Commission for the Blind. She attended classes on how to write checks and how to navigate the kitchen with failing eyesight. Her devoted husband of 60 years found a new job for himself. He became the chauffeur for all her friends and began attending her Tai-Chi classes. Just a short time spent by her daughters coaching her contributed to her independence. Had her daughters and granddaughters not helped her and supported her, she may have not been as independent.

Many aging mothers love hearing about their daughters' lives. They receive much nourishment from conversations about their work, their family, their travels, and new foods and the latest technology. The care provided by their daughters is special, and a mother may guard from introducing anything unpleasant when she is with her daughter for fear of isolating her. Many mothers receiving care from daughters are concerned about "talking too much." A daughter who once did not know how to boil an egg has different choices from those her mother had, options that may have contributed to her becoming the first person in her family to get a professional degree, for example. She may be feeling guilty about not spending enough time with her children and now has the demands of caregiving for a mother who is ill. In some cases generational differences cause daughters to say that their mothers were so needy that there was never enough time spent with them and that they "talked too much." When a daughter feels that a mother is controlling, she unintentionally criticizes her mother. This criticism is one of the most painful for an ailing mother. Sometimes mothers hesitate and cannot answer directly to a daughter's questions, or it may be that they simply cannot remember. Any criticism when one is ill only exacerbates forgetting. For example, Mary, a 75-year-old widow, explains,

> My daughter and I were always very close. She always told me everything. until she got married. When she shares things with me like the new house, her dog, or job, I get much pleasure from hearing about them. I feel like I am part of her life. I never tell her this because she is so busy and always in a hurry. Of course, I have been forgetting things lately, so perhaps it is my fault.

Many daughters told me that they did not realize how much their mother enjoyed being a part of their lives. Some daughters enjoy listening to stories about the past by mothers as it gives them a sense of history. Many, however, experience ambivalence about having a mother call them and talk on and on about her every ache and pain. Many daughters are aware that their mothers are aging and love to spend time with their mothers, especially when they know they may not have many years left. There is always a sense of connection between mothers and daughters when one is able to spend special one-to-one time with each other.

Many women I have known have expressed a sense of great pleasure when they have realized a sense of connection and sameness. Bridget describes the pleasure she got when her daughter Rose took her to Ireland for her 75th birthday:

> Going to Ireland for me at this age with my daughter was the best present I ever received in my whole life. We revisited every shrine, church, and sacred place that we went to when she was a teenager. She and my other girls complained then that I was dragging them to many museums. I knew it might be the last time in my life I would be seeing my beloved Ireland, and it was wonderful having my daughter treating me so special. Best of all though, I had my daughter to myself for a whole week. Now that is the best.

Her daughter later pointed out to me that she was having a wonderful time with her mother in Ireland, and when she realized "it was the same thing my mother did for me when I was a rebellious teenager," a sense of identification and connection with her mother was so meaningful that she said she hoped her daughter would do the same for her some day.

COMMUNICATION . . . AND MISCOMMUNICATION

"I don't want to ever make my daughter feel sad," said Mrs. A, age 84. She told me that her daughter did not understand her. "Even though I'm sick, she calls me once a week and thinks that's a lot." On the other hand, Mrs. A will not answer the phone in her hospital room because "it was probably my daughter calling." Mrs. A. said when she talked to her daughter, it brought her down. "She's always asking questions, like, What did the doctor say? Did you go out today? Have you gone to the hairdresser this week? Did you take your medicines? What is Dad doing? Does he exercise?" Because of a serious illness, Mrs. A is very vulnerable and also very critical of her daughter, who in fact is very supportive. She was also grieving the loss of good health.

Mrs. A interprets her daughter's interest as controlling and as a sign that her daughter thinks she is incompetent. On the other hand, Mrs. A's daughter feels as if her mother is controlling her by not answering the phone. She also places great importance on the questions she asks her mother and feels it "helps her to remember" as her memory is failing. In other words, what appears controlling to one person to another is being supportive.

As I spoke to the daughters of many of my patients, it sometimes seemed as if they spoke a different language from their mothers. Deborah Tannen, in the book *You're Wearing That?* says that a way to understand these differences between mothers and daughters is to understand the distinction between messages and metamessages. The message is the meaning that resides in the dictionary definitions of words. Everyone agrees on this meaning. In the conversation between adult daughter and elderly parent, they are communicating; but people frequently differ on how to interpret the words because interpretations depend on metamessages—a metamessage is the meaning learned from how something is said or from the fact that it is said at all. Emotional responses are often triggered by metamessages. Everything we say has meaning on these two levels. In the situation with Mrs. A, when her daughter called and checked on what she was doing and tried to connect with her (her daughter was in a hurry, had many things to do, and was just checking in to make sure her mother was OK) Mrs. A heard disapproval and control. Her mother heard the metamessage and jumped to conclusions. Perhaps this way of communication went on from the day her daughter was born and has a long history—we do not know—but when a daughter is in her midlife, and her mother is old and ill and may be by acting as if she wants attention or is somewhat demanding, the daughter should look for the metamessage. For instance:

Angela says to her daughter, "Did you go to Anthony's parent–teacher conference this week?"

Beatrice, the daughter, replies, "Of course I did. What do you think, that I'm a bad mother?"

Angela is asking for information so that she can be a part of her daughter's life, which is the message. Her daughter Beatrice interprets the question as an insult to her motherhood, the metamessage.

A caretaker daughter is finally taking a vacation with her kids and husband. She is leaving her mother for the first time in a year. The mother is not happy about her daughter taking a vacation and leaving her to be alone but wants to express love to her daughter.

Mother: I'll miss you this week.
Daughter: Ugh, Mom, you don't have to make me feel guilty about leaving you.

The mother may be taken aback by her daughter's response. She was just extending her feelings that she will miss her daughter. The daughter, on the other hand, feels criticized for taking a vacation and leaving her mother alone.

Chances are, you cannot teach your mother not to use metamessages. You can talk about it, but chances are they will remain. Although Angela is displaying care for her grandson, her daughter Beatrice is taking it as a personal insult.

> The metamessage of caring and criticizing is bought with the same verbal currency. But each party to the conversation sees only one. Daughters feel unjustly criticized, and mothers feel unjustly accused. When tempers flare, both feel blindsided. Neither sees the fastball coming because they're focusing on different balls. To the daughter, the criticism causes her outburst. To her mother, the outburst comes out of the blue because she believes in her heart that her intention was not to criticize, much less to wound. (Tannen 35)

Many of the aging mothers I spoke to about their daughters said they felt emotionally close to their daughters but wished their daughters were not so emotionally distant. What they meant was that whenever they talked to their daughters about things that mattered to them, the daughters acted as if they had more important things on their minds, and that their daughters' busy lives left little time for them. Daughters, on the other hand, discussed their mothers' unrealistic wants—visits or calls every day. So how do daughters and mothers at the critical time in their lives, during caregiving and care-receiving, solve this miscommunication? First of all, trust yourself that a good conversation can take place. Secondly, if your recent visits with your mother are not enjoyable, try taking her out on an outing or shopping day. Find a way to enjoy the visit. Distract her if she is critical by talking about something you know will interest her.

TIPS FOR MOTHERS AND DAUGHTERS

It is important to remember that the relationship with one's mother is one of the most influential relationships in our lives. Patience is key in many relationships, but for the mother–daughter bond, both patience and trust are key.

Remember that even while trying something different, many of us like to keep old behavior patterns that are familiar, and it may take some time to get used to a new idea. Talking to your mother or daughter in a new way can be quite an adventure. Learning a new way of communicating with your mother can also open up new conversations with other loved ones in your life. Changing the conversation with her mother may be one of the most difficult things a daughter does. Reframing a mother's comments from criticism to expressions of caring can change everything. Conversations between caregiver and care-receiver can improve a relationship once you change the script. One way that works for many women when talking to their mothers is reframing how they think about their mothers. This reframing of your thoughts often leads to talking to your mother in new ways. Do not react to a criticism; try to change the conversation. Your mother may not be able to react to you in her old way. By talking in new ways, a daughter or a mother can help the other change the conversations in new ways. In caretaking an elderly mother who may not live long, a daughter could remind herself that her mother is the keeper of myths and traditions and that these mothers carry within themselves the family legacy.

The fastest way to induce stress in your life is cutting all ties to your mother. Long-term consequences of not trying for a better dialog or just plain talking with your mother are feelings of anger and bitterness. Anger and bitterness lead to pent-up stress and manifest themselves in other relationships years later. Sometimes we all say silly things either to protect or to express concern. In situations that do not change, a daughter or mother will do more good by saying less, listening, and then going out for a long walk. For the aging mother, this action of not trying to understand and keeping silent can lead to depression at the end of life. Old patterns of behavior are hard to break.

When the caretaking role is seen as a burden by an adult daughter, she will have less of a positive view of her elderly mother. A negative feeling toward an elderly mother may be an attempt to ward off future loss when the mother dies. This is a defense mechanism that is not protective for either mother or daughter. In the past century, the view possessed by many psychologists has been that women must sever the attachment to their mothers in adulthood. Aging mothers internalized these views, and until the theory was turned on its head by feminist theories, younger women did not understand why this should be. Why should this be? This is a daughter's struggle, and supposedly the mother knows nothing of what is going on. When mothers do become aware, and do not discuss it because they do not understand it, they often retreat into ill health or become tyrants. In other instances aging mothers withdraw to avoid conflict and slide into a depression.

The daughter must remind herself, as she struggles to balance her life, that it is her choice to take care of an ill elderly mother. By making the choice hers, a daughter can fully appreciate what she is doing. She must make the caregiving her choice. Also, the aging mother must work to find a good support system other than her daughter. Without a support system in place, mothers and daughters will struggle and feel isolation. It is not the focus of this chapter to identify the issues that went on prior to this last stage in a parent's life. Though the popular press suggests that adult behavior patterns are established in early life, Karen L. Fingerman found that mothers and daughters in her study did not seem to view their current relationships as relics of their past experience. Rather, they remember changes in their relationships with "some periods more conflict-ridden than other periods" (Fingerman 2001, 101). Betty Brillo, for instance, never in her life got angry at her daughters and admired them her whole life (circumstances of her generation), and during caregiving for her husband, she reported in her diary that she was angry at them even though she knew they were devoted and did as much as any daughters could. She described these feelings as irritations, yet she still loved her daughters and family. At the end of her life, she wrote her daughters letters, apologizing for not being open and showing more affection to her children because "that was the way I was raised."

The History of a Mother–Daughter Relationship

Though my research shows that stress between mothers and daughters correlated directly with the mother's physical or cognitive decline, Karen L. Fingerman, in *Aging Mothers and Their Adult Daughters,* tells us that ambivalence between aging mothers and daughters is apparent long before the mother's health declines (7). Her studies examined the tension between healthy aging mothers and adult daughters. She reports that the strongest mother–daughter relationships maintain strong ties that stem from their shared experiences as women.

The Aging Daughter

Regardless of their geographic location, daughters are more likely to maintain strong ties to their mothers. Many of the anecdotes that I heard from daughters during caretaking were that they felt close to their mother, were still influenced by their mother, and felt guilt when she was critical of them and happy when their character was confirmed. On the other hand, many daughters felt stressed juggling the responsibilities of caretaking with their own autonomy. Though they love each other, mothers and daughters change the perceptions of each other, and as they age, daughters may have changed, and mothers may have not.

In the case of anger, aging daughters can use their anger as a tool for change when it challenges them to become more of an expert on the self and less of an expert on their mothers. In chapter 2, the daughter who said "shoot me first" before she ended up like her mother was angry. Many other daughters I met were angry too, not at mothers but at circumstances that they felt were out of their control. When one daughter had to place her ill mother in a nursing home, she did not turn the anger she felt onto herself; instead, she began doing whatever she could to expose the conditions that her mother had to endure before she died. She waited until her mother passed on before writing a blog on the Internet to expose the nursing home. Daughters can speak out about abuse and neglect reported in some institutions.

In the future, caregiving daughters will be more likely to be old themselves, struggling with declining resources of health, money, and energy. The social role of modern women, who are struggling with their own interests, obligations, and constraints, can lessen the supportive role of the daughter.

What the daughter can do: Change the conversation and replace old communication patterns. If there were difficult relationships prior to caregiving, things may not change. Think of this powerful vision: As you look into your own face, can you find yourself as her daughter, as an aging woman? If your mother has been your guide, can you see yourself becoming her guide as she ages? If she is ill, remember she is living in the segregated and secluded world of the sick, and you her daughter may have to help her navigate her way through a passage that you someday will face. Rebel against mediocre care and let your voice be heard.

THE ELDERLY MOTHER

An elderly mother may have learned very early in her life to keep her needs to herself. Many mothers feel that in order to protect their daughters, they should not give them bad news, and they need encouragement to be open about their own feelings. Many daughters complain that their mothers devalue them, and because there is a close relationship between these two feelings (loving and devaluing), it may be difficult for an aging mother to understand that devaluation of a daughter may be because she is envious. The defense mechanism of envy is very insidious and often provokes silence. As long as the mother devalues her daughter's accomplishments and never complains or compliments and says, "Everything is just fine," the mother wards off her own envy. Understanding this allows the daughter to have a different point of view regarding her mother. Yet a mother offers sustenance to her daughter in many ways that are silent and that are good. Offering nourishment by food, for many elderly mothers, has been their opiate for most of their lives. It starts at the breast with feeding her child, and somehow for some, it just went on and on. Elderly mothers ward off depression by immersing themselves in a busy life instead of expressing feelings. Elderly mothers want to keep in constant contact with their daughters. There are few social guidelines for daughters and mothers during caretaking activities. More than most men, women in later life, when dislocated from their homes, have reactions of grief, manifested in feelings of painful loss, somatic distress, and a sense of helplessness. In many cases the nursing home is not the answer, and also the options are not at the daughter's home. The options are in the community, and it takes a family member to research them. Include your parent in the planning and decision making regarding their care as much as possible, but understand that caregiving decisions are never easy, and plans to provide care may need to change.

If a mother is still married, she may be a caretaker for her husband and most likely her own parents. It is possible she is burned out. Caretaking a spouse in old age is laborious, and many women neglect themselves. For the generation of mothers in their seventies and over, new conversations may be difficult to begin, but think about this: if you can talk to your own daughter about things that are important, why not your mother? Mothers can maintain an independence by taking care of themselves first and then affirming their preferences and having conversations with their daughters regarding their needs before a life event occurs. Martha Stewart recently experienced caregiving for her mother, who died at 93 years old. When she was asked if her experience with her mother as a caretaker caused her to have any conversations with her own daughter, she said,

> If I have an ailment or a problem, I will mention it to my daughter. Like yesterday I said my back is still hurting and she said, "Well Mother, I feel sorry for you, but you have to lose weight and you have to do maybe a different kind of exercise." And she was right about all of them. But she is really smart that way, and she really cares about physical exercise. (Greene 2008, 4)

TIPS FOR DAUGHTERS

There are a number of things daughters can do and consider to enhance the experience for their mothers during caretaking:

- Make caretaking your own decision.
- Reciprocity is the key when it rules the relationship—think compassion and empathy.
- Set ground rules and limits in loving ways.
- Take a break as often as you can.
- Do not withhold information—sometimes shielding your mother from difficult news hurts her, but most mothers can take the truth.
- Trust yourself about what to reveal.
- Just because your relationship with your mother growing up was strained does not mean it will be the same now.
- Apply lotions and brush hair.
- Tell your mother how much you appreciate her.
- Reminisce about good memories. Let her tell her story.
- Buy your mother a DVD player and some of her favorite movies.
- Get her something you know would make her feel good about herself: a new necklace or a new shirt, for example.
- Get her a food you know she loves.
- Look at photo albums and reminisce.
- Demonstrate trust, attentiveness, responsiveness, and encouragement of independence.

- Turn to relatives, friends, and colleagues for support—we are all in this together.
- Giving back may just free you of old resentments that have kept you emotionally apart.
- Reflect, respect, reciprocate.

TIPS FOR MOTHERS

- Sometimes you have to muffle your own criticisms—know when to butt out.
- Do not offend.
- Maintain close ties with your daughter(s).
- Do not offer advice unless asked.
- Act sage-like at all times.
- Respect and reciprocate your daughter's privacy.
- Be direct with your communication and then move on.
- Do not be intrusive.
- Tell the truth about how you feel.
- Praise your daughter in good times and in hardships.
- Accept the fact that your daughter cannot meet every single one of your needs.
- Do not get under your daughter's skin by not thinking before you speak.
- Keep a friend.
- Computer-savvy mothers—send a quick "Just saying hi. Love, Mom" note.

Remember an Old Basque Saying

Show up
Pay attention
Tell the truth without blame or judgment
Do not be attached to the outcome

8

A New Life Passage

Our attitudes toward the future play a central role in the probability of achieving certain goals in life, and for many, one of the goals in later life is that caregiving will not be a burden, a burden that in some cases projects that the future holds little promise. If the caregiver is hopeful that his plan of action will be successful in meeting the goals of caregiving such as maintaining human connection, mitigating loneliness, dispelling myths, and keeping a loved one safe and reasonably happy, it will be successful. However, if the caregiving role is taken on with a sense of hopelessness where failure is always anticipated, then caregiving does become a burden. Furthermore, of central importance is that the caretaker's belief in one's own efficacy to attain such a goal gives rise to a feeling of competence—the capacity to make things occur. This belief that we can influence events gives one a feeling of self-esteem. When the caretaker feels helpless and hopeless, her usual skills and actions are no long effective for reaching a goal, and she may give up pursuing what she truly holds dear.

Thus, it is suggested that a new life passage that represents psychosocial rather than intrapsychic attributes between a care-receiver and caregiver as a continuation of the life cycle, based on Eric Erikson's famous work *Childhood and Society,* in one sense feeds psychoanalytical thinking from the mechanistic "cause and effect" thinking that did little justice to either nature or destiny in man. At the heart of his work in chapter 6, he develops "Eight Stages of Man." When he speaks of a cycle of life, he actually means two cycles in one:

> The cycle of one generation concluding itself into the next, and the Cycle of individual life coming to a conclusion. If the cycle, in Many ways, turns back on its own beginning; so that the very old become again like children, the question is whether the return to a child likeness seasoned with wisdom—or to a finite childishness. That is not only important within the cycle of individual life, but also within that of generations, for it can weaken the vital fiber of the younger generation . . . Any span of the cycle lived without vigorous meaning, at the beginning, In the middle or at the end, endangers these sense of life and the meaning Of death, in all whose life stages are intertwined. (133)

Between the stages of adulthood and old age, I argue that a new stage is evident. The new stage is caregiving and care-receiving. A person's strengths at any of Erickson's eight stages are the following:

1. basic trust versus mistrust
2. autonomy versus shame and doubt
3. initiative versus guilt
4. industry versus inferiority
5. identity versus role confusion
6. intimacy versus Isolation
7. generation versus stagnation
8. ego integrity versus despair

Caregiving and care-receiving are part of the life cycle, and just as we recognize the stages of childhood, adulthood, and old age, this stage should be recognized because all of the person's identity and sense of values must be summoned up to cope with pain, terror, betrayal, loneliness, and death.

For Erikson, the cogwheeling stages of childhood and adulthood are truly a system of generation and regeneration. He contends that human evolution has arranged it so that humans have a long childhood and then a long period of generation, so that adults are then prepared to be for their children what is needed at the evolutionary or cultural moment, or at a moment in history. Adding a stage called "caregiving" will complete the life cycle in a more meaningful context. What this requires is a recognition that it is part of the life cycle, so that in future generations, a person's strength will be recognized in such a way that productivity and creativity are enhanced and arranged for. In the last stage of one's life, old age, one looks back and weighs one's life. The judgment for a person who has taken care of people and things and feels nurtured until the end leads to self-respect. When an individual develops a chronic or physical illness, the problems in identity in death are heightened and compressed. We need all the resources of our personal identity and our sense of values to cope with pain, terror, depression, and death.

We all establish bonds to others somewhat like we did in childhood. These bonds, once established, are persistent. The crucial one is that between adult and child and of child and adult.

9

OURSELVES REDISCOVERED

True manhood consists in realizing your true self and restoring the moral order or discipline. If a man for one day realizes his true self and restores complete moral discipline the world will follow her. To be a true man or woman depends on yourself, what has it got to do with others.

—Confucius, *Analects*

Though caregiving interrupts our lives, this process can trigger a spiritual awakening within us in which we discover what is truly important in life. We cannot solve all the problems of caregiving for good. It is not even desirable because thinking this way makes it impossible and traps one in the process. Life is a process of development and change, which should not end until the last day of existence. In caregiving the opportunity of reinventing yourself is all around you. A turning point may come when you realize that no amount of devotion can take away your loved one's pain and sometimes suffering. Or when you think your own life will end because you are too tired or exhausted. Or when you say to yourself, *I feel like an orphan* and *Am I next?* Or when a spouse dies, and as a widower, your life seems to have no meaning.

For example, the hospital chart revealed that Tony was an African American who had served in World War II and was a war hero. He was admitted with pneumonia after being found by his daughter in bed at home unresponsive. His wife had died six months before. He had three adult children and many grandchildren. His primary physician referred him to me for social support. I found Tony crying when I entered the room. He said he wanted to go home. I assured him that it was our goal to get him home when the pneumonia was under control. This seemed to motivate him to talk more. He revealed that he missed his wife of 60 years and felt "life was over" for him. He admitted to feeling depressed and was able to recognize that he was mourning. He received a great deal of support from his family and talked about his married life and how close he was with his grandchildren. Tony did not feel he needed intervention from our behavioral medicine department, and I continued meeting with him after he was discharged from the hospital. I met with his children, who agreed to provide support, and they revealed that they did not know how their father would manage without his wife. Tony raised many issues during his six-week course of grief counseling. One was his fear of going to "the veterans' nursing home" and being "put out to pasture." One day, Tony came in excited and very animated; his children had given him a computer, and a grandson had begun teaching him how to use it. He began sending e-mail notes to his grandchildren in college. Every day he would send them "the word of the day." He was delighted when they answered him back. Eventually Tony started volunteering at the veterans' hospital near his home. He became a central and welcomed figure to the disabled patients. He began taking the men who had no families on outings to lunch and museums. Tony never gave himself enough credit for being able to handle life's problems in new ways, but he told me the most useful thing for him was the fact that he could master technology and could now keep in touch with his grandchildren and many of his war buddies. In his last e-mail to me, he wrote that he was writing his memoirs of World War II for his grandchildren.

Caregivers and many others of us like Tony never give ourselves enough credit and see that we in fact can grow in spite of a crisis that suddenly emerges. When a situation, such as a parent reaching a critical phase in their illness, arises, we cannot think of anything else. Creativity takes a nose dive, and there never seems to be enough energy. Caregiving can infuse all of life if we allow it to. We are meant to continue being creative, and during caregiving, we must be aware that many powerful and gentle changes can happen. The Talmud reads, "Every blade of grass has its Angel that bends over it and whispers grow, grow." When you feel the emotional toil of caregiving, do not tell yourself, "I can't do it anymore"; try to step beyond this feeling. Some form of prayer usually gets you to the other side of fear. Do not worry about what everyone will think or say if you take a week off and have some solitude. Paint or draw or scribble something you may have dreamt about. Pablo Picasso said, "Painting is just another way of keeping a diary." These tools may strike you as being a diversion, or as a denial of what is happening in your life, but they are not. You are nurturing your inner well. It begins with a process of revision, and if we pay attention, you may have to dig yourself out of your old self to become your true self.

Many of us strive all our lives to truly be ourselves, but at this stage of one's life, the striving can take place internally. This internal striving comes from the fact of being a caretaker. Because so many feelings from within others and us take place in caretaking, they are easily internalized. It may be a period of moratorium for some; it seems as if you are getting nowhere, your goals are on hold, and it is still unclear what your aim in caretaking will be. Think of it as a task, as preparing for rediscovery. We should caretake another human because caregiving is good for the soul. It is another form of self-expression.

The caretaker undertakes caring with no agenda in mind. Having a novice's happy mind allows one to challenge some of the old rules of caretaking.

Each situation of caretaking is unique and reveals to us if we really listen to its own rules. In caretaking you are doing two jobs: one is taking care of someone else, and the other is taking care of yourself. In caretaking one can heal the fear or shame in past failures. In re-parenting a parent, we gain compassion. When caretaking extends over a long period of time, spirituality or religion becomes the only thing you can rely on. Faced with illness and change, we want to curl up and cry our eyes out. I call this a spiritual awakening because these cries come from the soul. They remind you that you need to be nurtured. They remind you that taking care of yourself means you cannot wait to find more time for yourself; you have to make it and take it. No other person can make time for you. People make more time in the morning, in the doctor's office, on a plane, at lunch, at a coffee break, at the hairdresser, at the barber's, or while brewing tea. Steal the time if you must, and suddenly you will realize you have time.

The trick is to make time for yourself in the life you already have. Moaning that you cannot find time for yourself is a lie you may be telling yourself. These lies cause envy, anger, and cynicism. Do not be a bystander in your own life. If you are angry, know that you're angry and do something about it. Acting out like a teenager or two-year-old has nothing to do with spirituality or knowing your true self. The caretaker is observing a true, real story. As a witness to another's life, the heartbreak of loss, how another person copes, you are building your own castle again and filling each room with compassion and strength and refurbishing yourself. How you live in this new castle depends on you. It does not depend on anyone else. You may be also writing your own true narrative as an older person, with dual responsibilities in a fast-paced world filled with uncertainty. Think of yourself as a multifaceted human being. Take a 15-minute break and benefit from whatever you do. Remember, whenever you go into each room of your castle, "there you will be" alone with yourself.

Because anxiety and burnout are often high in caretaking, particularly over a long period of time, we may get into difficult situations in the relationship where the self feels out of balance and you are at the bottom of your selfhood scale. When this happens, it is difficult to stay connected to anyone, and it is impossible to speak directly to your own issues. Often the caretaker becomes so focused on the care-receiver that the care-receiver becomes selfless himself and cannot make clear statements about what his needs are, and difficult issues are not brought up or discussed. In many instances they are replayed in the daily struggles, and anatomy becomes destiny because the ill person feel worse.

Let's face it: you will not get an Oscar for caregiving. Fame and glory will not come to caregivers who strive to keep their lives in balance and who refuse to neglect important relationships. What do you get? Private rewards that enhance the self. The changes you make during this relationship may leave you frustrated and scared and many times may separate you from your friends.

I recall a meeting of my support group, and when we went around the table sharing what was the scariest thing about having a chronic illness, people had concerns over how the people they were friendly with before getting sick were slowly changing their attitude toward them. A filmmaker said, "I was the top guy in my circle of friends. I always got free tickets to movies for them and their families and sent gallons of popcorn to their homes. I might have been a show-off, but all I wanted was to share some of my luck. Some of these same people who live in my condo avoid me."

When I asked what they had discovered about themselves by having a chronic illness, most of them said that chronic illness had taught them humility and that the greatest assets that they had were their family. Most of the men in the group responded to my next question about attitudes toward themselves by reporting that having a positive attitude helped them solve many of the frustrating problems they faced because of illness. Many of the woman said negative things about themselves, such as, "Well, I do not think about myself," and others said, "I just feel lost and helpless to do anything positive."

This experience in the group, together with many others, changed me and moved me professionally into a different phase of helping people. Prior to that I wanted some patients to rid themselves of things like not talking to their mates or demanding too much from themselves. What I really wanted was for everyone to get along and help each other. What came about because of this change was that I focused more on the positive aspects of who these people were. We did some role playing, and because I brought treats and fed my group members every month, we shared "cookies and drinks." Eventually, the shift I had hoped for began to take place in the group. People started to be more open, more like their true selves. They looked forward to each other's ideas and suggestions, and they began nurturing each other. They became less negative toward themselves. This is not to say that negative behaviors are bad because many times, they serve their own positive purposes. For instance, one person in the group was always negative and very confrontational. From what I put together, it was her method of seeking attention and being heard. Eventually, the group pulled together, and as they became more tolerant of her attention-seeking strategies, she stopped engaging in them.

After many years, this group became very cohesive, and substantive changes occurred. They were now caretaking each other. Change did not happen with a big bang or angry confrontation. What really happened was that people began to trust themselves and feel safe, and from small manageable baby steps, change took place. Many of my patients were experts at giving and doing for children, spouses, and friends. They learned that being responsible for themselves was important in discovering their own strengths. Vito began cooking his own breakfast instead of complaining about what his son prepared for him. Sara went back to playing bridge and started a carpool so that she did not have to drive every week. They had regained some of the self-respect they had always had and had stopped blaming others for not giving them "respect." Illness can be an opportunity for caregivers and care-receivers alike to rediscover themselves. Rediscovering ourselves by caretaking means you may have to change some attitudes and behaviors. Change requires courage and planning and discipline.

If you have carved out a true and authentic self and are happy and content and do not want to change, don't. If you do not have the will to change, then don't. If, however, other people and other people's wishes and values define who you are, then caregiving is an opportunity to define and rediscover your true self. It is a difficult and often risky challenge. Becoming a true, authentic self means that we can pretty much be who we are instead of what others expect us to be. Do not, however, try to change the person you are caring for. They too, like some of the patients in my support group, need to recognize that they want to transform themselves. In the caregiving relationship, the care-receiver has so many needs and wants that the situation is more complex. But truly being who you are brings more of a self to the relationship. Everyone pays a price when we betray and sacrifice ourselves.

No one else can tell you if you need to make changes. But most people are very intuitively wise. Whatever you come to the caregiving situation with has served a purpose for you in your lifetime. Respect that part of yourself, and because you are the best expert on your own self, no one else can tell you what changes you need to make and when is the right time. Caregiving is a time of transition, and transitions are difficult because they make you face the unknown. When a crisis arrives, it seems that everything is at stake, and people tend to choose to stay stuck in the thinking they know. Transitions in caregiving are teachers, and when we avoid the task of learning about our-selves in time of transitions and caregiving, we do not do "God's work." In the beginning and in the middle of caregiving, you may not be able to think about yourself, but give yourself time. You will be ready when you are willing to try a number of approaches that best suit your needs. When the time comes to commit yourself, sagacity sets in, and all sort of things happen. And when that happens, it will affect your emotional well-being, your sense of self. As Confucius says, what does it have to do with others?

10

ANXIETY, STRESSES, AND STRAINS OF CAREGIVING

The stresses, strains, and conflicts often cause the ill parent to be a tyrant and the adult child who is caregiving to be unable to focus on anything else. Coaching the caregiver and care-receiver with a stress-reduction plan may reduce many of the aspects of helplessness and hopelessness that interfere with successful transitions in later life.

Years ago, I attended a lecture on stress by Dr. Herbert Benson, who is affiliated with the Benson-Henry Institute for Mind Body Medicine. He had just written a book, *The Relaxation Response,* one of the first books of its kind. Benson described how our blood pressure, heart rate, and breathing adjust to stress. Everyone has an innate defense mechanism against excessive stress, he argued, and one then limits the negative effects of stress by decreasing heart and breathing rates, lowering metabolism, and allowing the body to reach a healthier state of being. Benson called this reaction the "relaxation response" and suggested it could be used as a tool to promote good medical care. Many in the audience, all doctors and nurses, were skeptical. Many medical professionals have no doubt that stress plays a role in illness, but the audience was skeptical about the existence or relevance of the relaxation response. Benson's lecture confirmed for me what I had observed for years—that stress can exacerbate illness. What will the doctor find? Will my loved one be able to return home? Will they die from this? Will he be disabled? How will we cope? Although often unspoken, these fears are common to most.

Research shows that 60–90 percent of visits to physicians are for ailments associated with stress, such as headache, pain, or stomach problems. For example, Ann, who has been a caregiver for 6 months, had never taken a sick day in her 14 years of working. But once she started caregiving for her elderly father, she made several visits to the emergency room. At one time, after an argument with her father, she slipped and fell on the ice outside his home. Fortunately, she suffered no ill effects from this fall. Her last emergency room visit, however, resulted in an admission to a hospital. Ann thought she had the symptoms related to a heart attack, but the doctors confirmed that her symptoms were stress-related.

In short, caregiving is a stressful experience, and learning how to minimize or alleviate that stress is essential for the well-being of the caregiver and care-receiver alike. Often the demands of caregiving cause caregivers to neglect their own needs and their own health, but for people to be effective caregivers, these issues cannot be ignored.

Caregiving is a stressful event whether the caregiver is an adult child or spouse. Recent research reports that the stress affects other members of the caregiver's family too, including secondary caregivers, children, and grand-children.

By the time of Dr. Benson's lecture, I was already using relaxation techniques to help many hospitalized patients and their families reduce their stress. Many of the elderly were not convinced that a simple technique such as deep breathing would help alleviate their anxieties. In those instances, whatever seemed practical or understandable for each individual became the mechanism for a relaxation technique. This included prayer beads, rosaries, and sometimes prayer. One woman undergoing tests for breast cancer would recite *The Rime of the Ancient Mariner* as her own form of relaxation. I read everything I could on helping people reduce stress. I attended workshops and tried everything on myself. I created a relaxation tape called Waves of Relaxation (see appendix). For years I have observed that in conjunction with relaxation techniques, verbalizing stress has a positive effect in releasing some of its pressures and tensions.

WHAT IS STRESS?

We all feel stress, but how can many of us define it? Stress is the body's automatic physical and emotional reaction to a demand placed upon it. It is most often caused by change, such as loss of a loved one, job or career switch, illness, injury, vacation, demands, or lifestyle changes. Stress is not always negative. Stress is part of our daily lives and can be a challenge. Just the right amount of stress can spur you on and stimulate you. Different people perceive stress differently. Excessive stress affects our body and the way we react to a situation. We may feel anxious, hopeless, angry, worried, unable to concentrate, and sometimes unable to make decisions. When our body is unable to adapt and cope in our environment or in social situations, we are distressed.

Stress is always accompanied by changes in body chemistry. We produce adrenaline and other stress hormones that can trigger muscle tension, an increase in blood sugar and blood production, and a rise in blood pressure. A hormone named cortisol is released by the adrenal glands, affecting muscle tone and nerve tissue and increasing gastric acid secretion. If the stress from a highly charged experience becomes a constant occurrence, the immune system is compromised. When minor hassles continue for long periods of time, such as reacting with irritability and frustration to every minor stress or complaint from a loved one who is ill, the caregiver's tolerance for stress is decreased. Over long periods of time, stress can become chronic.

Sufferers from chronic stress associated with change resulting from caregiving pay a high price by feeling helpless, hopeless, and out of control. Most of us experience crisis situations that seem burdensome or overwhelming; eventually the crisis is over, and we breathe a sigh of relief. Think about taking a test for something very important in your life, how your thoughts could have been way out of control before and after taking the test. Once the test is complete, and you have passed the examination, you regain your sense of relief. Taking on caregiving, however, is not like taking a test. It can take months and sometimes years. Be forewarned about your loved one's illness and ask the doctors to make realistic predictions about your loved one's prognosis. List out commitments, both for you and for others in the family. Talk to other members in the family. If family members will not help or understand what you want to do because of prior family relationships, find other sources to help out. Spell out specifically what you need. Martyrdom and self-sacrifice in caregiving will only contribute to stress and anger.

Strong feelings such as anger, anxiety, and helplessness are common. Turning these feelings inward to yourself will cause confusion, and these feelings, if denied, will drive your behavior. When you are already exhausted and feeling drained and depleted, this stress can lead to illness. Caring for a loved one takes a toll on both the caregiver and their family. In my study, adult children reported that not only the ill parent but also other members in the family required more emotional support because of a parent's illness. I found that the psychological strain of having an ill parent contributed to a caregiver's negative self-image. The issue of a negative self-image may have come up because of the sudden responsibility of caregiving placed on the adult child who did not know what to do. For these reasons it is important to explore strategies that will deal effectively with stress.

Caregivers' stress is both emotional and physical. Research suggests that caregivers are more likely to have health problems like diabetes and heart disease and often suffer from burnout. Demands involved in juggling caregiving, a job, and parenting can require time, great effort, and hard work. Stress related to change can lead to illness.

Acknowledging one's stress over caregiving or care-receiving is essential to controlling it. Denial will only increase susceptibility to illness. Each phase of the caregiving–care-receiving relationship has its own stresses and strains. In the early phase of caregiving, there are numerous decisions that need to be made depending on one's role and position in her own family. For many women, the decision to become a caregiver when they are pursuing a career or advanced degrees while raising children may have a profound effect on their marriage. Illness of parents or illness within one's own family, children leaving home, and retirement are likely to create more stressors in the family. In sum, each phase of caregiving has its own pressures and strains. These stresses will impair the caregiver's capacity to deal effectively with the problems encountered in caregiving.

When we are under strain, we are more apt to lose our temper and become irritable, which can lead to faulty thinking and excessive anger. Other effects of stress include forgetfulness, withdrawal from friends and partners, anger, and childish patterns of thinking.

When you are becoming "stressed out," the first advice is to try to avoid becoming stressed in the first place. *Easier said than done,* you say. Because we cannot eliminate stress, we can change the automatic way we think about stress. First, recognize that negative statements and thoughts cause negative actions. When negative thoughts become automatic thoughts, whether they are misconceived or not, you believe them. Recognizing that these thoughts are self-defeating and many times irrational will help you stop, think, and choose the way you want to respond to a situation. Recognizing your negative automatic thoughts helps you to challenge and restructure them. For instance, if your parent or loved one is in a miserable mood whenever you visit her, you feel frustrated and angry, saying to yourself, *The least she could do is be happy to see me.* You may act on this misinterpretation by being negative and unreasonable with her. If you are able to resist the temptation to portray your mother as miserable and inconsiderate, and find out what is bothering her at this very moment (and it could be anything), you might come to the conclusion that you were inconsiderate and consider another explanation for her mood. Then you would realize that your frustration and anger were unjustified. You may have been depressed in that moment, and by checking this out and not jumping to conclusions, you avoided the negative image. The following principles by Aaron Beck, MD, found in the book *Love Is Never Enough,* will help you understand.

1. We can never really know the state of mind—the attitudes, thoughts, and feelings—of other people.
2. We depend on signals, which are frequently ambiguous, to inform us about attitudes and wishes of other people.
3. We use our own coding system, which may be defective, to decipher these signals.
4. Depending on our own state of mind, at a particular time, we may be biased in our methods of interpreting other people's behavior, that is, how we decode.
5. The degree to which we believe that we are correct in divining another person's motives and attitudes is not related to the actual accuracy of our beliefs. By using the preceding principles, you may be able to define your automatic thoughts, which will then change the way you think and behave. Negative thoughts have the power to make you stressed. Head off your negative thoughts by countering them with rational responses.

When you are already stressed, there are steps to minimize the impact of stress on you and others. Recognize the signs: tension; irritability; being prone to overreaction, misinterpretation, or jumping on people who want to help or offer advice; and irrational beliefs such as "I have to love my loved one without ever feeling anger no matter what happens—I have to be perfect in everything."

Be alert to symptoms to stress. Are you tense? Are you eating too much or not at all? Has your blood pressure or cholesterol risen rapidly? Are you irritable? Are people in your family telling you that you look exhausted? Any of these can be suggestive of stress. Other symptoms may include headache, inability to sleep or excessive sleep, impotence, anger, hyperactivity, anxiety, lack of concentration, crying, fatigue, impotence, forgetfulness, an increase in general negativity, and feeling out of control.

I used to demonstrate what happens with stress to patients who were hospitalized and in my support groups with this exercise. Try this right now. Clench your hand and fist. Notice how blood flow has almost stopped. Release the fist and notice how blood again enters and relaxes the hand. Other parts of the body—such as the muscles in legs; the tension and tightness in your face, head, shoulders, and neck; and a knot in your stomach, for example—react the same way when we hold onto stress. The body becomes tense and seems to become one giant knot. Your hand, as in this example, feels cut off from your body. Chronic stress cuts you off from your body and mind. Beside the physical changes, your thoughts and emotions will be affected.

These physical manifestations of stress are called the fight or flight response. The same reaction occurs in animals. When animals are faced with a threat, they either face the threat and fight or run to save themselves. Many problems posed by an aging ill parent cannot be resolved by fight or flight. It is impossible to fight a parent who will not adhere to a medical regime. On the other hand, abandonment of an aging ill person is out of the question. Caregivers who face this kind of situation every day use the term "double bind," coined by psychologist Gregory Bateson. The daughter of one of my patients asked me, "Do I pick up my child from school because he has a slight fever or go to the hospital to see my father-in-law who fell in the kitchen?" These situations have the potential to be very stressful.

The ramifications of chronic stress for the caregiver are terrifying. Caregivers are at a high risk for a multitude of psychological and physical ailments, including anxiety, depression, heart disease, high blood pressure, diabetes, and cancer. This is not only a result of the physical toll of caregiving, but also from intense emotional reactions experienced during the process. According to the AARP, people who are providing care to an ill person have more family feuds, have more accidents, and make more trips to the emergency room, to hospitals, or to a family physical exam. Researchers found that people who report high stress in their lives are twice as likely to develop diabetes within eight years of caregiving activities. Studies reveal caregivers of a parent experience symptoms of depression at twice the rate of the general population. Caregivers frequently neglect their own health when caring for others.

Enza was caring for her husband. She did not have the focus or the time to cook for herself, and she began eating more and more fast food. She also did not feel that she had the time or focus for exercising. At her own doctor's appointment, her doctor warned her that her cholesterol and blood pressure had risen significantly. She ignored her doctor's warning to eat better and take care of herself better. Enza suffered a small stroke a few weeks later and developed diabetes in the hospital.

Caregivers like Enza worry about whether they can continue to care for loved ones and at the same time manage their own anticipatory grief over the death of their parents or loved one. Some caregivers have a fear of getting sick themselves and become unable to fulfill their caregiving duties. They may have other stressors such as job insecurity and financial problems and must take the time to find a way to reduce and understand their anger and feelings of guilt. Caring for a spouse may be the contributing factor in becoming a victim of caregiving and not taking care of yourself.

When caregiving is a part of your life, there are many changes. Daily life might need to be restructured because of time limitations. Cooking, cleaning, shopping, paying bills, driving patients to appointments, and picking up prescriptions are all time-consuming. Some caregivers report devoting 12 to 40 hours a week to the basic needs of the care-receiver. All of these demands are laid on top of one's existing obligations.

It can be overwhelming to take care of another's bladder and bowel functions day after day. It is tough to bear the angry moments when you know you are trying the best you can to help your loved one have some sense of dignity. The adaptation for a caregiver to this kind of change causes distress for many people.

Stress also influences other people close to the caregiver. The care-receiver can also feel especially stressed when being cared for. It is difficult to lose one's independence. The indignities of wearing hearing aids, using toilet commodes, wearing incontinence pads, and needing help with personal care are difficult to accept for some, particularly for those who have been independent for the majority of their lives.

When one practices stress relief, the immune system is best prepared to protect the body. Highly charged situations prove to be manageable with a clear mind. There are many individual differences in the way one reacts to a stressful or frustrating event, but the key for everyone is to interrupt the negative cycle.

We have to recognize signals of stress in our body. Does our heart begin to race? Are we clenching our fists? This is the point at which to stop the stress cycle and choose best how to calmly handle the situation. Small changes may seem insignificant, but for instance, if you can visit your loved one every other day instead of every day, this may make a big difference in the amount of stress you have in your life.

DEFEATING STRESS

To defeat stress, we must take personal responsibility—we control our own bodies and minds. Stress management requires both body and mind. We all possess a natural protective mechanism against stress: our mind. Our thoughts can help us create and induce a feeling of calm and relaxation in our body.

We always talk to ourselves. These thoughts as we talk to ourselves are called "self-talks." Self-talks can be very helpful in defeating stress because the conversations we have with ourselves are always going on. Caregiving and illness can lead to much emotional upheaval. Strong emotions produce physiological roller-coaster signals. As difficult as it is to maintain a positive attitude, we may feel anxious and incompetent. Try different techniques to see what works best for you.

The benefits of reducing stress are innumerable. With a recharged and stress-free mind, both mind and body will function more effectively. Coping skills will improve. In caregiving as in life, you have a choice—to defeat stress or to let it defeat you.

One of the most important ways to control stress is to find or build a support network. Support from others helps when we are under stress. Support can come from a variety of sources, such as a spouse, siblings, psychotherapists, church groups, family, and friends. We feel better, and our minds and bodies work better with a support network. It is difficult to stay motivated and positive every day. Some days, you just want to crawl into bed yourself. The stresses from caregiving are not always amenable to the physical reaction of fight or flight. There are times when you cannot take a day off or run away. Talking it out with someone is beneficial and offers relief from the loneliness of caregiving. A good cry with a friend can lessen the stress. A secondary benefit from talking it out is that you can hear a different perspective from someone who is not so involved. Support from others makes your life richer and connects you to a larger community. Studies show that people who feel supported have more energy. Receiving support and nurturance helps you to give it. You are cared for and can care for someone else. It may be hard to "open up" to someone else. By "opening up" I do not mean to burden people with your problems, but instead just to be honest. Hearing yourself say "I just cannot do this anymore" can sometimes open up new possibilities. Sometimes it makes more sense to seek professional help from a counselor.

You will have more energy when you feel supported by others. Our primary support, however, comes from within ourselves—from the way we talk to ourselves. One of the phrases I refer to often is "negative thoughts lead to negative action." Negative actions and the automatic thoughts that come from talking to ourselves can become self-fulfilling prophecies. If you are constantly thinking "doomsday-type" thoughts while you are caretaking, you become overwhelmed and stressed. One of the ways to stop negative thoughts and negative self-talk that can lead to these "doomsday thoughts" is to question them. The next time you catch yourself with negative thoughts that cause you stress, stop and think, "Are these reasonable or just my feelings of anger and being overwhelmed that are making me think this way?" Stopping to restructure your negative thoughts is one of the most powerful ways of reducing stress.

One technique for changing the way we automatically talk to ourselves is cognitive restructuring, based largely on the work of Dr. Aaron Beck, as mentioned earlier.

We often jump to conclusions or imagine "what if" scenarios. What if Mom falls at home? What if she breaks her hip? What if she cannot take care of herself after that? What if I need to hire 24-hour care? Those catastrophic scenarios produce anxiety, which is a counterproductive reaction. It only upsets us further. Here is an example of one of my patients channeling her stress in a more positive manner:

Sally goes to her mother's house daily after work to inject her mother's insulin. Sometimes, Sally gets stuck at work and arrives late at her mother's house, much to her mother's ire. Sally became so stressed by her mother's criticism that just the thought of going to her mother's home made her heart race and blood pressure rise. One day, Sally's mother began yelling at her for arriving late for her injection. Instead of yelling back as she usually did, Sally took a deep breath, stepped back, and decided not to overreact to her mother. Sally decided to change the way she had been reacting to her mother's negativity. She stopped her automatic assumptions that her mother was extremely negative when things did not go her way. She put herself in her mother's shoes and realized how important the insulin was for her mother, who sat there waiting and watching the clock. Sally began complimenting her mother on the many positive things she did for herself. Except for giving herself the insulin injections, she was quite an independent lady. Eventually, with Sally's suggestion, her mother began knitting again and watching the weather report every evening to keep her updated as to the temperature for the next day. Within a few months, Sally's mother learned to give herself the insulin injections.

Some caregivers turn to medication for help with the emotions and stress. Many doctors will prescribe tranquilizers at the mere mention that one is struggling in their caretaking duties. In some cases, medication is an important health need and is beneficial as long as it is monitored properly.

Continue with your life, whatever you do. Take vacation days. Contact home-care agencies to research their services. If you decide to hire someone to provide caregiving for a few days a week, ask your siblings to contribute monetarily.

It is sometimes difficult for caregivers to admit they need help. Asking and getting help is an important step in taking control of the situation. For instance, when finances are not available for paid help, ask a friend or a sibling to call or check in with your parent twice a week. Caregivers are not weak for admitting they need help. Would you rather be prideful and miserable, or give your loved one the best care-receiving experience possible? Merely reading a caregiving book can be comforting. Caregiving books provide tips and resources for further exploration. It is reassuring to know others *do* share your experience. There is hope in the situation.

Do you remember back to your high school chemistry days, about potential and kinetic energy? Stress is potential energy. That energy can be expended through physical activities such as walking, gardening, sports, swimming, singing, dancing, and jogging. Yoga and Tai Chi are both activities that exercise the body and mind. Exercise can improve cardiovascular fitness, respiratory capacity, and strength. It can help lower blood pressure, raise HDL ('good') cholesterol levels, relieve emotional stress, and help with weight control. Weight-bearing exercise (such as running or walking) may delay or prevent the bone loss that comes with aging (osteoporosis). At the very least, these activities can serve as a distraction from stress.

MIND AND BODY

Now that we know the mind and body are connected, we are able to examine the concept of mind–body healing. Peace of mind is an enormous part of feeling physically well. Mind and body experts such as Herbert Benson, MD, have found that stress can trigger a physiological process that directly raises susceptibility to disease. Emotions influence immunity, and furthermore, positive emotions may bolster your immunity, whereas negative emotions will depress it. A buildup of unaddressed stress may be related to the breaking down of the body's natural defenses. Just as radios, instruments, and cars must be tuned to perform well, so also do one's body and mind.

One way to strengthen our peace of mind is mindfulness. Mindfulness is the practice of experiencing life moment to moment. Originally a custom of ancient Buddhism, mindfulness is an excellent way to be aware of all that we have and slow down our hectic lives. It does not matter what religion, if any, you practice, because mindfulness is a completely secular idea. When our primary focus is on the here and now, we can give all of ourselves to the moment and the activity in which we are involved. Ellen Langer, in her book *Mindfulness,* describes mindfulness this way: "when one is mindless there is a focus on outcomes—the categories and patterns that were created prior [to] mindfulness. In contrast to mindfulness, mindlessness is a state of reduced cognitive activity that results from reliance on a rigid structure that may arise after several repetitions of an experience" (72).

We can be mindful of both the physical and the emotional. We can heighten the experience of physiological sensations and be further aware of impending signs of stress. Mindfulness allows us to be cognizant of our emotions. Are we overreacting? Could we handle the situation better? Mindfulness is especially relevant while caregiving. Though we cannot always be mindful, caregiving is a situation in which mindfulness can help us make better decisions for both the care-receiver and ourselves.

The opposite of mindfulness, mindlessness, is common in the lives of the elderly. According to Langer and her colleagues in the article "Old age: An artifact?," "the physical and social environments of the elderly tend to encourage mindlessness." She relates a study performed in a Connecticut nursing home. Patients who participated in making minor decisions for themselves and who were given something to be responsible for (in this case, a plant) were happier, more active, and more alert than those who did not make any decisions. More so, the members of the group with choices were over twice as likely to still be alive a year and a half later.

The loss of independence and not having a voice when entering a nursing home lead some patients to feel incompetent and unimportant. The patient will often internalize this negative self-image, and an overwhelmingly negative cycle is created. Almost all sense of purpose for the care-receiver is eliminated. This is blatantly observed in nursing homes, where our loved ones have little, if any, control over any daily activities. If someone you love resides in a nursing home, try introducing whatever form of relaxation they might follow. Prayer is easy for elderly people regardless of religion. Giving a loved one a plant to watch over provides them with a connection to you and gives them a daily chore.

RELAXATION

Unlike pharmaceutical therapies, relaxation techniques pose no physical or emotional danger. Relaxation techniques have proven effective without the need for medication or special experience. A special effort must be made to experience relaxation. Many say they just cannot find the time. It is something that can be done without the help of others. Even brief 2- to 10-minute relaxation methods practiced several times a day can help with the buildup of stress. Mini-relaxation techniques can be done any place and anytime—while waiting in the doctor's office, waiting in line for medications, or sitting at your desk. Take the time to relax in-between commercials.

Relieving stress by using a relaxation technique can help lessen and even eliminate the discomfort of stress-related symptoms. The more you use a relaxation technique, the more you will recognize your own particular signs of tension. The body holds these tensions. As in most situations, one must practice to be truly successful. This must happen when feeling bad *and* when feeling good. It is easy to say, but harder to do. It you find it hard to take time in the midst of a busy day to relax, try waking up a few minutes earlier. Relaxing in the morning sets a nice tone to the day.

Bud's family was organized around his illness. His family monitored his blood sugar, ferried him to doctor's appointments, waited with him for laboratory results, and cooked special meals while trying to keep him occupied. Every day presented a new crisis and challenge due to his kidney trouble, diabetes, and high blood pressure. He was unable to walk by himself. He had been receiving dialysis treatment for five years. The relaxation response and some coaching helped Bud get the courage to communicate to his wife and daughters that he was ready to stop dialysis treatment. This meant he would die. The family was able to work out a schedule so that he was never left alone for the remaining weeks of his life. Support and relaxation brought them closer together because they had been so busy caring for him that they had forgotten their own relationships. I learned this a few weeks after his funeral. Most of these feelings went unexpressed for many years during his illness. The family later became involved in caring for their mother who died two years later.

Breathing is an important component of relaxation. Many of the strategies I discuss are influenced by breath. Every time we breathe, we expel carbon dioxide and inhale oxygen, renewing ourselves with every breath. Breathing slowly will set the pace for our heart rate and calm us down. Because breathing is an involuntary process, we hardly ever notice our breathing—it is usually something we take for granted. But learning the proper way to breathe enhances other relaxation methods. Belly breathing can be done sitting, lying down, and walking. Have you ever noticed that breathing rapidly from your chest brings more anxiety?

Relaxation is just one step on the path to feeling good. Positive imagery is another component to successful relaxation. Sit in a comfortable chair and close your eyes. Put your feet up. Where would you love to be right now? Out in the country, smelling the grass and the clean air? With your toes buried in the sand on a Caribbean beach? Sipping hot cocoa in front of a fire in the middle of winter? These are all calming thoughts.

Remember the Little Engine That Could? He used positive self-talk to help him through an experience. "I think I can, I think I can" affirmations can help control stress. Some examples of positive self-talk are "I can do it," "I am capable," and "I am strong." It might help to write affirmations on paper and post them in places around your house. They might be the little push you need during the tough times.

Humor is a stress buster for the caregiver and care-receiver. Norman Cousins wrote that "hearty laughter is a good way to jog internally without having to go outdoor" (*Anatomy of an Illness* 84–85). A good belly laugh is good for you and when you think of it all your internal organs get a workout. A good belly laugh ignites the soul. Most people feel a new excitement. Some expectations get fired up after a hearty chuckle. Notice faces of the elderly after a good laugh—they actually look younger. Physically, people relax when they laugh and become responsive. Laughter decreases blood pressure and stimulates circulation. It serves as a workout for the heart muscles. Laughter can also decrease levels of the stress hormones adrenaline and cortisol, which narrow blood vessels and reduce immune system reaction. Additionally, laughter decreases dopamine production, which stimulates the fight or flight response.

Find anything that makes you laugh. In this age of the Internet, cable TV, and DVDs, there are a plethora of ways to keep ourselves entertained and laughing. If you are not naturally one to laugh, it is something that can be developed by reframing one's thoughts. Humor will give pause in your daily routine to step back and enjoy what you are doing. It will help you further enjoy the time you spend caregiving for your loved one. After a good belly laugh, you may actually see the world differently. Among other benefits, humor can be used to bond the caregiver and care-receiver.

Humor does make a difference in one's approach to a challenging situation. We all have a conscious decision to either laugh at stress and adversity or fold under its weight. Enjoy the time the care-receiver has left, no matter how long it is. If anything, humor gives us the comfort that we are bringing joy to a situation.

In my personal and professional life, I have learned that relaxation, in its many forms, is necessary to alleviate the pressure and stress of caregiving. All it takes is a willingness to try.

STRESS HARDINESS

It is possible to argue that with appropriate relaxation techniques, one can become "stress hardy." Suzanne Kobasa and colleagues defined three components of stress hardiness—commitment, challenge, and control. Herb Benson's group added closeness as a component, and I added my own addition, community.

- *Control.* As a caregiver, one needs to have a sense of control in life. Be aware of the many personal choices one can make. Control, whether perceived or real, seems to make a difference in the way we respond to stress.
- *Commitment.* Be involved in the loved ones' care. Show them unconditional love and let them know you will not abandon them. Successful caregivers experience a fullness of purpose.
- *Challenge.* Acknowledge the challenges of caregiving and be proactive when facing them. It is difficult to be proactive when facing these challenges. Challenge your loved ones when they say they cannot do something. Think of the word *crisis* in Chinese, wéi jî. It is made up of two parts—"danger" and "opportunity." Stress-hardy caregivers are not afraid to create new opportunities. Opportunity can come out of challenge. Let anger challenge you to become an expert on yourself instead of on the one you are caring for.
- *Closeness.* Being close to the care-receiver can create a feeling of safety. For yourself, it is important to keep up close relationships and social support.
- *Community.* Caregiving takes a whole community. Keep friends, neighbors, and relatives close, learn from them, and each day find someone who will make you laugh. Join a caregivers' support group and the National Alliance for Caregivers. Neighbors and friends are willing to help, but you need to be explicit in telling them what you need.

34 Strategies to Control and Combat Stress for Caregivers and Care-Receivers

1. Avoid caffeine, alcohol, and drugs.
2. Get up 15 minutes earlier in the morning. You will have more time for normal morning activities as well as time for anything that might come up unexpectedly.
3. Write things down. Do not leave things, such as appointments, to memory.
4. Make copies of all keys. Carry a duplicate key in your wallet, apart from your key ring.
5. Be prepared to wait in doctors' offices. Bring a book or an MP3 player with you.
6. Procrastination may seem tempting, but you will have better peace of mind if you get things done as soon as possible.

7. Allow 15 minutes of extra time to get to appointments. People who are ill need more time for walking and getting ready, getting out of the car, and walking to the office.

8. Make sure your loved one carries a card with your name and number, his or her medications, his or her address, and a second emergency contact number. You should carry one also.

9. Do not strive for perfection. Just do your best.

10. Count your blessings. There are many things to be thankful for.

11. Ask questions at doctors' appointments. Try and anticipate any issues that might arise.

12. Say "no" to extra projects and other things you know you do not have time for.

13. Try to stay organized. This will make things easier for you in the future.

14. Monitor your body for stress signs.

15. Keep a journal. Writing feelings down can be cathartic.

16. Keep a positive attitude. If you are primed for success instead of failure, you are more likely to succeed.

17. Do not give up on taking care of yourself. It is important to still take pride in one's appearance.

18. Work on one thing at a time. When you are working on one thing, do not think about everything else you have to do. You will do a better job at the one thing you are doing.

19. Delegate responsibility to capable family members.

20. Sometimes, swallowing one's pride might be the best thing to do. Not every argument is worth trying to win.

21. Make a conscious effort every morning to give yourself an affirmation that caregiving will not get you down.

22. Try to maintain a healthy diet. Healthy foods will make you feel better. You will feel more energized. Certain foods, especially those with magnesium, vitamin B, vitamin C, and folic acid, can help combat stress. Some of these foods include blueberries, chickpeas (or hummus), almonds, fish, lentils, clams, and whole grains.

23. Try to find some time everyday to take for yourself. This can be spent meditating, reading, or doing absolutely nothing at all.

24. Purposely include humor in your life. Sometimes it will not come in by itself, so you might have to seek it (e.g., watch a comedy).

25. Sleep is crucial. Sleep is your opportunity for refreshment and renewal. Without sleep, it is hard to operate with a clear mind.

26. Exercise! Exercise stimulates endorphins, which make you feel good. It also improves circulation. At the very least, it is a distraction and may improve self-esteem. Something simple like walking or running does not even require a gym membership.

27. Avoid those who are negative. Similarly, avoid negative self-talk (e.g., I'm a bad caregiver, I didn't do enough).

28. Give yourself praise. Caregiving is a hard job. Pat yourself on the back.

29. Schedule things to look forward to. This could be a movie night with your family, dinner with an old friend, a visit to a museum, or a quiet night of relaxation in the tub.

30. Slow down. Use your brain to calm your body.

31. Try not to criticize others. Focus on yourself. See the good in people.
32. Prioritize. The lawn does not necessarily need to be mowed today.
33. Do not cut off loved ones. Stay in touch. Alienation will usually make stress worse. Often a best friend can help as much as a therapist.
34. Reward yourself with something special. Schedule a manicure, or buy that CD you have wanted.

The information I have presented might be a little overwhelming. It is your choice to follow all, some, or none of my suggestions. Be creative to use a technique you come up with that has meaning in your life. We can coach our loved ones on stress reduction and encourage practice. Teach your loved one a short relaxation technique that he or she can do on a daily basis. Or explain to him or her that beading (rosary beads, prayer beads, any beads) can be very relaxing. It worked with many of my patients.

11

Voices of Grandchildren

My grandmother might try to do more than she is capable of. She is impatient and wants things done "now." I am the only grandchild who lives in the area. If my aunt who is her primary caretaker gets sick and not around to care for my grandmother, I worry that my grandmother will wither away.

—Sally, granddaughter, age 21

As the questionnaires from my research at the Lahey Clinic piled in, I began to realize how much grandchildren worried about their grandparents and their parents who were caretaking. Though none of the grandchildren in my study provided direct care to their grandparents, many of their parents did. I wanted to find out what grandchildren were thinking about their elderly grandparents. My research was an outgrowth of the research by Albert Bandura, who observed that people's perceptions of their capabilities affect their behavior, and adult children did not perceive their elderly parents as positive; as a result these adult children suffered anxiety and helplessness. Gerontologists had come to the conclusion that helplessness—being unable to control or affect one's own life—is the key to decline. A number of studies indicated that the feelings of helplessness might be associated with a poor survival rate for those under medical care. I was looking for a way to help those adult children who felt helpless during caregiving for an elderly parent. When grandchildren visited their grandparents in the hospital, even grandparents who were critically ill tried to smile and engage in conversation. Grandchildren's presence lit up the room. They seemed to give the grandparents hope.

Mrs. Santiago's granddaughter came in one day. After tapping her grandmother on the leg, she took her face in both hands and kissed her and said, "Hi, Noomi. It's me, Betsy." Mrs. Santiago forced a smile, which led to her being fully awake and acting full of confidence about her upcoming hip surgery. "I brought you your favorite lemon tart," Betsy chirped and proceeded to cut the lemon tart in half and serve it to her grandmother. Mrs. Santiago told me later that she always smiles for her grandchildren. Betsy seemed scared when she sat down. Mrs. Santiago said, "She talks to me like my little girl," and when Betsy left, she said to her grandmother, "Everything will be OK, Noomi, and when I come back to see you, you will have a new hip. You will be the bionic woman. Then we can walk together." This led me to decide to add grandchildren to my next research project.

My research had centered on adult children and elderly parents and indirectly on what others had to say about caregiving. As I talked with grandchildren, it seemed to me they were the carriers of generations of sustenance, and I wanted to help them be aware of this. The opinion of grandchildren seemed to be a missing link. I had no intention of bringing them into the fold of caregiving by having them take on any of its responsibilities. With the increase of life expectancy, shrinking family size, the increase of dual-earner households, and the increase in multigenerational families, this made sense to me. I had witnessed so many other grandchildren being with grandparents on one of their last happy occasions before dying. For some grandparents, the voices of grandchildren are the "breath of life" part of them that we do not see—"the soul." Grandchildren remind us that we are more than our genetic makeup, even more than our life stories. Often they bring us back to our childhood, and we recognize where we have been and who we are. They are the future caregivers.

Not all grandchildren fit one mold, but grandchildren offer new ways of thinking, and they are fun. Small grandchildren become adult grandchildren who can open bright new worlds for grandparents as they develop into the next generation. Many grandparents serve as trusted allies and confidants to grandchildren. Although some grandchildren seek out Eastern gurus and Zen masters, their grandparents are in the kitchen with wisdom that often goes unnoticed. In mostly all cultures, grandparents pass traditions on. A prudent grandparent prepares for the second trajectory in life. To know how to grow old in spite of ageism, and to foster rewarding relationships with their adult grandchildren, is indeed is a role that can inspire them to feel more confident because the grandchildren in my study were very positive; for everyone who took the time and effort to answer my questionnaire there must be thousands more.

THE RESEARCH

One hundred alert and oriented elderly (randomized) hospitalized patients, 75 years and older, participated in the research. A social worker helped the patients fill out a 20-question survey that asked them to answer how well they thought they would perform once they were discharged from the hospital. Would they be able to get their own meals, dress themselves every day, go to the bathroom by themselves, and take their own medications? And if they needed help, they were asked to rate their degree of performance from 0 (could not at all) to 100 (could do fully) if they could rely on help from family, children, grandchildren, and friends if they became sick. The social worker determined the functional status of the patient and asked whom they perceived as their main support person and names of any grandchildren. The adult children and grandchildren were asked to fill out a similar questionnaire that asked how confident they felt that their elderly relatives would be able to perform daily tasks of living once they got home, such as getting meals, getting dressed, and doing housework, and that asked who the elderly person could depend on if help was needed. Most grandchildren's responses were very similar to their grandparents' answers, but the adult children seemed less confident in their parents' ability to care for themselves. The following case is an example of many of the respondents:

Mr. Santora was a 79-year-old widower whose wife had died three months ago and who had been admitted for acute cellulites. He had gone to stay with his daughter as a temporary measure after his wife died, and then he became ill. This was his second admission since his wife's death. He had visiting nurse services while at his daughter's home. He used a walker and had many medications, including Coumadin, which must be regularly monitored by a nurse. Mr. Santora was somewhat depressed but alert and oriented. He often used humor as a defense. He had three adult daughters and eight grandchildren. He wanted to go back to his own home upon discharge. To complicate matters, the utilization review board in the hospital informed him that his insurance would not cover an acute stay in the hospital. He agreed to go to a facility that would be covered by his insurance. The family was still mourning the death of their mother and grandmother. The day before Thanksgiving, a daughter called and requested that he go to her home for Thanksgiving because it was his birthday. The visiting nurse was contacted, and the nurse reported that because the service knew the patient, they would service him with nursing, home health aid, and physical therapy as long as he stayed with his daughter. They felt he was too sick to be alone and would not provide care if he went home. The family was totally overwhelmed and asked me to continue searching for a nursing home for him because his widowed daughter was in the process of selling her home and moving to a small apartment.

Mr. Santoro's daughter had very low expectations of her father's ability. His granddaughter Gail, a 27-year-old mother of two small children, wrote on her questionnaire that her main concern was that her mother, aged 47, was "burning out" because of the stresses on upon her from caregiving. Eventually Mr. Santoro was placed in a nursing home, and he lived there until he died. His granddaughter was worried about her mother because she had become depressed.

Voices of Grandchildren

Ann, who is a 20-year-old student, said she had major concerns that her 85-year-old grandfather might not be able to get help in an emergency because he lived alone. She would try to call him, but if he did not answer, then she would call her mother, and everyone got "stressed out," so she stopped calling.

Beth, a 24-year-old secretary, was 90 percent confident that her grandfather would remain in his own home. Her father, who was an only child, had no confidence that his father would be able to be independent his own home. Ironically, the patient, who was 87 years old, had a 90 percent confidence that he would do well at home.

Shawn, a 19-year-old student, said his grandfather was well taken care of by his grandmother, who was "quite remarkable." He lived within 10 miles of his grandparents and kept an eye on them. He shoveled the driveway and sidewalk during winter.

Jane's granddaughter, a 21-year-old paralegal, reported that her grandmother could count on her at least 75 percent of the time if she needed help. Her mother, Mary, said that Jane could not count on her grandchildren.

Dora, a 23-year-old receptionist, said, "My father moved into my grandmother's home to take care of her when he got divorced. My grandmother has a very short attention span and I worry about the two of them. My grandmother depends on my father and is very stubborn about having help in her home. She is agoraphobic and my father is freaking out."

With greater life expectancy, American families will experience an increase in the number of surviving generations and also a decrease in the number of family members within each generation. This will greatly affect caregiving in the future. It is possible that grandchildren only 10 years from now may have the responsibility of caring for parents and very old grandparents. Though the grandchildren in my study had a more positive outlook on how their grandparents would manage at home when they went home from the hospital, they experienced stresses that trickled down from their own parents who were caretaking. These same grandchildren, who live in the shadows of the baby boomers, reported not having any experience with caretaking. For every grandchild who took the time to respond to the questionnaire, there are thousands in this country who may have the same concerns. Grandchildren want meaningful relationships with their grandparents.

A Granddaughter's Letter

Dear Gloria,

I am attaching this letter to my questionnaire. In writing it, I discovered something very precious to me. I am a graduate student in social work and plan on working in the field of gerontology.

My grandmother was short and chubby with a soft cuddly face, and she always had a mournful expression. I am much taller than her, and I loved to stand next to her while she cooked steak and onions for my father and five other robust sons. When I was thirteen years old, my grandmother and I went to Washington, DC, by train to visit my uncle, who was then a lawyer. The brown paper bag she carried smelled spicy and pungent, filled with foods my uncle Mark loved. I was not too happy with those smells, but today, I look for them. Since we had never been out of our small town, my grandmother was dressed for the occasion in a blue dress and a black felt hat that had blue flowers on the brim. The flowers matched her watery blue eyes. I remember looking at the sturdy black laced tied up shoes and said to myself, "I will never wear those kinds of shoes."

My sojourn with my grandmother put an end to the only world I knew. It changed me because I was so protected by my family that I was very shy. My uncle took us to all the sights, and one day my grandmother and I went on a bus trip by ourselves. My grandmother was not fluent in English, so I was her guide. She smiled and nodded, and today I think she was pretty cool wearing those sturdy shoes because we walked miles.

On the train ride back home, my grandmother talked mainly about how important marrying the right person would be in my life. She had five daughters-in-law. She told me of someone who was very special in her life, St. Theresa of Avila—who was a mystic. My grandmother's interpretation of St. Theresa was that she "closed her eyes so she would not see what she could not tolerate"—I did not understand what she was trying to say then, but as I went on with my life, St. Theresa kept coming up. George Goethel, a professor at Harvard, put me on to St. Theresa while I was in college. He reminded me about something I already knew. My grandmother may have misinterpreted St. Theresa's real message, but I like to think this is the way she survived in a world that was different than the one she knew. This passage has a real message to all peoples. "I do not know if I have explained it clearly, self-knowledge is so important that, even if you were raised right up to the heavens, I should like you never to relax your cultivation of it; so long as we are on this earth nothing matters more to us than humility and self knowledge," she said. My grandmother grew up with the stories of St. Theresa that she heard from her own grandmother.

I saw my grandmother often before she died. She introduced me to many other stories, stories with unforgettable maxims on love, respect, and also suffering. I am not sure you will quite understand what I am trying to say. But when I come to turning points or crises in my own life, I think of my grandmother first and then the story of St. Theresa. For me what matters is that my grandmother's life does not serve as a model for my own. Only her stories do that. You cannot make up stories like hers; you can only live by them.

What I discovered that is precious to me is that in many ways I am like my grandmother, and I know I will always have a part of her soul in mine.

Good luck on your research.

Best.

12

A Good Death

If it is the way of nature that we not "encroach on another" (and simple observation confirms that it is), then nature must of necessity provide some means of certainty that we, like Homer's leaves, progressively attain a stage at which we "drop off, and make room for another growth" . . . Scientists of every stamp have attempted to identify the mechanism by which living things do this, and we still don't know for certain what it is.

—Sherwin Nuland from *How We Die*

Death belongs to life as birth does. The walk is in the raising of the foot as in the laying of it down.

—Rabindranath Tagore, from *Stray Birds CCXVII*

This chapter describes the impact of caregiving on the dying process. Those who caregive have an unusual opportunity to forgive their parents or spouses for what happened in the past and make peace with them. Letting go of old resentments and anger helps one accept the fact that no one has the perfect parents. When the wound of childhood goes too deep, the best solution is not to provide primary care to one who is dying.

If anything in the world is certain, it is that we will die. No matter which ethnicity, race, or religion, poor or rich, we all share that common covenant. Each family, culture, or religion has its own death rituals and traditions. As a generation dwindles, their traditions tend to disappear as well. Each generation develops new perspectives and new customs to add to or replace existing traditions. This is to provide our loved ones with the best circumstances possible in death.

Many forget that dying is a psychological process as well as a deterioration process. The dying person, even before disintegration begins, fears a plethora of things, such as loss of autonomy, disfigurement, becoming a burden, letting loved ones down, suffering, and the unknown. The dying person will never know what his grandchildren think of his dying. For the caregiver, the shadow of death shows that life is now measured, and time is much more precious. Deeper meanings and priorities emerge that make life worth living. As a dying person, to be in touch with the spiritual and enjoy nature, to leave a legacy for future generations, to heal relationships, to spend time with those he loves, and to have faith are important. The learning process for a caregiver and others is ongoing as new challenges and opportunities grow and develop.

Personal Stories/Grandfather/Grandmother

In thinking about this chapter and a good death, I went back in time to renew my kinship with my great-grandfather. I was eight years old at the time my great-grandfather died. I remember the intimacy and art of this memory, like an image from an old antique mirror. He said in his last days, "I do not want to die—Non vuol mori." These were my great-grandfather's last words before he died peacefully, as he was released from pain and suffering. I remember the scene of a great, very old, old man perched in his high bed with several pillows covered with white pillowcases. The linens were pressed and crisp. The comforter was covered with my mother's white linen sheet that she used on her marriage bed. Two clay pots held blazing red geraniums on the windowsill. The women would come and go, and there were always at least four or five matrons in the room. They were always praying while they tended to him, their prayer beads tucked into the pockets of their aprons as they spoke softly in Italian. During the last few days, each of the women held a white linen-covered spoon in his mouth gently, keeping his lips pursed and parted as he was gasping for breath. They were his human ventilator. I remember staring while the candles flickered angrily. I used to dream of the shadows they reflected on the wall. The matrons' gray shadows moved quickly, as they administered care and comfort. In my grandfather's final days, the men in the family came and went. The women stayed, maintaining the vigil, keeping the candles lit, sharing the responsibility of death. As the apostle Timothy fanned the flames of early Christians, these women were fanning the flame of caregiving and care-receiving. A red brick was kept in the oven at all times. The brick was covered with warm, white flannel and placed at the foot of my grandfather's bed to keep his feet warm. My mother told me then, "When you die, your feet get cold and stiff." The doctor came every day with a black suitcase. It seemed as if everyone in our Italian neighborhood visited one by one. My grandfather had run the grocery store in the center of the ghetto. Food kept coming to the apartment in abundance—lasagna, meatballs, and pasta. A cousin brought Chinese food in a huge aluminum pot, which made us all laugh. We had never had Chinese food before. The familial and informal network of no-cost respite care was traditional in this neighborhood. Family, neighbors, and acquaintances reached out in times of grief and provided sustenance for each other. My great-grandmother and other relatives would comfort themselves by talking to customers in the grocery store. Giving updates on her father's condition seemed to restore my grandmother, a solemn, stoic woman. My great-grandfather finally passed on a sunny Sunday. His red geraniums withered and faded soon after.

Today I ask myself, was this a good death? It was not in a hospital setting. No one was asking my great-grandfather to "let go." No one asked if he should be resuscitated; there were no papers to sign. Whatever drugs given to him by his doctor went unquestioned. Duties of the hospice were shared by a community of caregivers. There was the dignity, grief, and sadness of the women who came and went. When my great-grandfather said in his final hours, "I do not want to die," I believe that he did not want to leave the peace and tranquility of his little Italian ghetto where he was always present. He never gave up his ability to share his wisdom with the community, and in turn the community never gave up on him, even when he showed signs of dementia. As in his lived life, he taught us all many lessons that week when he died with such hope, courage, and engagement with his fellow man. These lessons prepared us well for the tragedies and suffering that come with living a life. The experience was unforgettable. I have carried this image of my great-grandfather all my life. Scary as it was when I was eight years old, today I realize that being part of his final exit made me aware of the sacredness of a life lived with meaning and purpose. I try to live day by day, trying to deal with pain and life's disappointments, knowing that peace and joy are within my reach. It is up to all of us to lay the groundwork for this future generation.

Good Death

Sogyal Rinpoche, in *The Tibetan Book of Living and Dying,* said, "There is no greater gift of charity you can give than helping a person to die well." It is the unalienable right of all of us to have or share in a good death, also called *benemortasia.* This term was coined by Arthur J. Dyck—*bene* meaning good, and *mors* meaning death. *Bene* in benemortasia is deliberately unspecified to avoid the declaration that a death must be painless or induced in order to be "good." Nothing in the Judeo-Christian tradition provides an exact blueprint for the most compassionate thing to do when someone is dying. What constitutes a good or happy death is a disputable matter to this day, leaving a certain vulnerability in the matter. Therefore, we use our best judgment and try to act in the wishes of our loved one.

Is a good death a universal wish, or is it just a formulation of words? Can we realistically hope to make people feel better while they are dying? Many terminally ill or chronically disabled patients report that besides the fear of pain and disability, fear of abandonment is high on their list. Mary, a 94-year-old woman told me, "What I fear most is being a burden to my children and being alone when I die."

At the last stages of life, what is a good death? If we were to live for 100 years, would we take 10 years of this to die? Will the people we love be there with us? Most of the patients I spoke with feared "death by intensive care" more than dying (Gross 2008). When an elderly person is near death, the tendency of caregivers is to protect the parent in ways that may not be beneficial for a good death. One main example of this is prolonging life using medical technology. This may lead to unexpected negative consequences.

Slow medicine is a course of treatment using less zealous health care at the completion of one's life. The Dartmouth Medical School originated the method when contemplating a typical course of action that may have "high risks and limited rewards for the elderly." This can mean rejecting hospitalization, a slew of tests, surgery, or medication. The concept of slow medicine aims for "comfort rather than cure." It is possible that invasive or extreme treatments can cause more harm than good. Instead, patients and their families who choose slow medicine hope for a calm and natural progression toward the end of life. The Dartmouth researchers argue that slow medicine may not necessarily change outcomes, but the patient who is elderly and has chronic or terminal conditions is saved from aggressive and unnecessary treatment as well as tests or intervention to delay death. There are many people who are eager for any and all intervention, however, and they are certainly entitled to this option.

Can we define a bad death? In a study done by Dr. Karen E. Steinhauser and colleagues at the Veterans Affairs Medical Center in Durham, North Carolina, the 85 participants easily described what they considered to be a bad death. This included untreated pain, aggressive short-term treatment, and feeling disregarded. In a bad death, decisions would be rushed, and families would be unprepared for death.

Where people die has meaning for themselves and their loved ones. Although most people would prefer to die peacefully at home, many are not that lucky. According to a study performed by the CDC, 56 percent of people die in hospitals, and 19 percent die in nursing homes. One thing we can do for the dying person is let her know how much she is cared for and that her life had meaning.

Some who are dying want to be informed of their situation. Others, on the other hand, just want hope, such as telling them they will be okay. When we falsely reassure others, we communicate messages meant to mislead them. What we ourselves do not believe cannot be hidden from the person facing death. We can mislead the dying person through gesture, through disguise, by means of an action or interaction, and even through silence. I do not imply that you intentionally lie to yourself or deceive your loved one. Many people I worked with in the hospital suspected that they were close to death, and some families, because of their values, could not acknowledge to themselves or to their loved one that death was near. Because of this denial by the family, many patients took longer to die.

My mother's insight into her dying was luminous. While in a coma, she sat up and asked, "Am I dying?" I told her she was very sick. She sank into her pillow and peacefully passed away. I did not lie to her and say, "No, Mom, you'll be fine." I know my mother would never have forgiven me for lying to her. Just as she would have wanted, the last words I spoke to her were the truth. Similarly, we can learn a great deal from the story of Ivan Ilyich. When

Ivan Ilyich went to the doctor, his doctor ignored Ilyich's inquiries about the severity of his illness. What tormented Ilyich the most was the deception. His whole family accepted the lie that he was not dying. His family was not willing to admit what they knew and what Ilyich knew as the patient. They wanted him to participate in the lie that he was going to recover. Left alone, Ivan Ilyich groaned not so much with pain, as terrible it was, but from mental anguish. He wept on account of his helplessness, his terrible loneliness, the cruelty of man, and the absence of God. In his last two weeks, he existed almost exclusively in his memories of the past, beginning with the present and working backwards to childhood.

> He, however knew, that do what they would, nothing would come of it, only still more agonizing suffering and death. The deception tortured him—their not wishing to admit what they all knew and what he knew, but wanting to lie to him concerning his terrible condition, and wishing and forcing him to participate in that lie . . . Apart from this lying, or because of it, what most tormented Ivan Ilyich was that no one pitied him as he wished to be pitied. At certain moments after prolonged suffering he wished most of all (though he would have been ashamed to confess it) for someone to pity him as a sick child is pitied. He longed to be petted and comforted. He knew he was an important functionary, that he had a beard turning grey, and that therefore what he longed for was impossible, but he still longed for it. (Tolstoy 1960, 137–38)

Ivan Ilyich gave up on himself, and his family gave up on him in a time when they needed each other the most. Unable to receive comfort, pity, or love from his family, friends, and colleagues, Ivan moves toward Gerasim, his servant, and renews contact with a fellow human being. Contrast this with the words of Dr. Thomas Graboys, a nationally renowned cardiologist who is battling an aggressive form of Parkinson's disease—"It takes a great self-discipline to be proactive when illness can be so diminishing, and it requires the support of those around you. If you don't want others—your family, friends, and caretakers—to give up on you, you cannot give up on yourself" (p. 185). This is a powerful statement not only for the caregiver and care-receiver, but also for all of us.

There is a great opportunity for bonding during caregiving. Little kindnesses offered to the person such as talking, touching, and praying are inspiring examples of the persistence of life in the face of death. Paint your mother's nails. Brush your father's hair. These small gestures can strengthen the bond between caretaker and care-receiver and give the patient an increased sense of self-worth and love.

This bonding is even possible with paid caregivers in hospitals and nursing homes. At the Lahey Clinic, I developed a "life review," which became a one-page biography added to the patient's chart. Physicians and nurses widely applauded the addition. In turn, the hospital staff developed an appreciation for the patients' backgrounds and were able to connect with them on a deeper level.

On the other hand, some caregivers make the dying process more stressful for the care-receiver. Surprisingly, I have seen families argue while their loved one is dying. I have had to pull them aside and say, "Your loved one knows that you are fighting. She will not die unless she knows there's peace within her own family. Do you really want her last memory to be of you fighting?" They showed little weeping or sadness, and it is possible that their hostility toward each other caused their mother much pain and restlessness and an unpleasant death. It is also hard for the dying to let go of life when there is conflict with close relatives.

Six elements of a good death were identified by a study at the Veterans Affairs Medical Center in Durham, North Carolina.

1. Pain management. Pain often triggers anxiety, which can make the situation worse.
2. Patients want a voice in courses of treatment.
3. Patients want to be informed about what to expect for the future.
4. A good death will provide time to review one's life, resolve conflicts, spend time with loved ones, and say goodbye.
5. Patients want the ability to determine what is truly important in life and to share those thoughts with others.
6. Patients want to be acknowledged as a person of worth and understood.

Elisabeth Kübler-Ross (1975) gave names to the five stages people experience after a terminal diagnosis: denial, anger, bargaining, depression, and acceptance. She argued that those who were able to reach acceptance were most likely to experience a good death and die in peace.

DEATH AND GROWTH

Not only can death be more meaningful, but Elisabeth Kübler-Ross argues in *Death: The Final Stage of Growth* that all of us are dying, not only in the final stage of life, but also after a divorce, a separation, losing a job, and the loss of good health. In dealing with these changes, we experience a cyclic course of death and rebirth. As a caregiver, you may eventually share in the death of your parent or loved one. Although the care-receiver may not be able to continue growing, the challenge for the caregiver is to be aware of the changes one has experienced during the process to further cultivate his own emotional development.

DEATH IS NATURAL AND DESERVES RESPECT/AGEISM

To make death a better experience for all, society must confront its fears and stereotypes about death. As a society, we need to acknowledge to ourselves that death is as natural as birth. We view death as a separate realm of our existence rather than a stage of life. Our society views death as the worst thing possible, but death is not the worst possible thing because it is part of the life cycle. We are born, we live, and we die. This is the natural order of things.

Some who practice ageism in our society believe that the old have no legacy and have finished contributing to society. Ageism has developed from the obsession to look young and be young. It is both latent and visible in our society. Are we sending the message to our elderly that it is preferable to die, instead of getting old and becoming a burden? Many of the fears and attitudes we have about death come from fears of our own mortality.

Our own fears of dying and preconceptions of aging can worsen aspects of one's aging process. In a society that is so youth-oriented, the second half of life seems full of deterioration. Author Nancy Osgood (1989) believes these feelings have been present since the ancient Greeks, who viewed aging as "an unmitigated misfortune and terrible tragedy" (29). Manhood in Greek time, as often in current times, was viewed in terms of physical ability. Mimnermus, a seventh-century B.C. Greek, wrote, "The fruit of youth rots early; it barely lasts as long as the light of day. And once it is over, life is worse than death." Mrs. Kiernan's story offered a 20th-century alternative view to such a grim ending in life.

The more we fear death, the more we repress it. We need to change the myth that dying is a tragic experience. In searching for new ways to abolish old age, we negate this stage of life that has meaning for future generations. We cannot always be there at the moment of death, but physical presence is not always what people desire. What they desire most of all is to know that an attachment figure is available. This feeling helps with the loneliness that some of us must endure in death. We can either make the decision to be morally responsible for each other or let our loved ones suffer and die feeling alone.

GRIEF

I would be remiss to omit grief in a chapter about death. *Grief* refers to the process of experiencing the psychological, social, and physical reactions according to your perception of loss. Grief is a genuine response to any loss or sorrow. *Mourning* is what we refer to as the conscious and unconscious process that gradually undoes the psychological ties that bind you to your loss. Mourning helps you to learn how to live with grief and how to live healthily in everyday life. None of us grieve in exactly the same way, but it is important for all us to remember that grief is an important experience in reaching acceptance and moving on. Importantly, the way a caretaker grieves will have a profound effect on that person's children and grandchildren.

Usually, the grieving person will experience feelings of numbness, shock, and disbelief (Janis 1971). The person may operate in a stunned and almost confused condition. Physiological symptoms, such as dry mouth, crying, and a poor appetite, may accompany the psychological demonstrations of grief. There is a need for safety, nurturing from others, and patience. Scattered periods of anger and blame may interject, often until the catharsis of a funeral. Regret and despair may follow. With some time, the grieving may subside to the point that daily activities can be resumed. There will still be some lingering sadness and periods in which the grief can return (Janis 179–80).

Many caregivers begin the process of grief on the day they decide to become caretakers. Mrs. Anderson started grieving when her husband was diagnosed with dementia. She told me grieving was "not new for her." Her father spent years grieving her mother's Alzheimer's until she finally passed from the disease. Mrs. Anderson purchased a cemetery plot for herself and her husband, prepaid for his burial, and gradually began the process of therapy. She moved herself and her husband to a condominium to lessen the burden of maintaining a house and joined the Wellspouse Support Group. When her husband died, she had steadied herself by seeking out positive people and making smart choices.

In the words of an old Italian Proverb, "Whoever forsakes the old way for the new knows what he is losing but not what he will find" (*Chi lascia la via vecchia per la nuova, sa quell che perde e non sa quell che trova*). Some people might feel it is necessary to address the death of a loved one in a way their parents and relatives have previously dealt with death. Feel free to keep some of the old traditions, but do not be afraid to add new traditions that might help you deal with the experience in a better way. *This does not necessarily mean to throw away old values.* For instance, when my brother passed away, it was difficult for me to go on with my everyday activities. My mother, on the other hand, would have made the grieving an everyday experience, staying at home all day, avoiding things that were "too happy." I know my brother would not have wanted me to experience his death as they did in my parents' generation. Therefore, after some thought, I decided to have my family together for a weekend away to celebrate my brother's life. In forsaking some of the old ways of my ancestors and adding some of my Jewish friends' perspectives on death and mourning, I was surprised that after my brother died, I could go on actually living. My own parents and grandparents could not go on with life, so they did nothing for a year, whereas I was able to go to my grandchildren's graduation and other sustenance-giving activities in my life. My brother, sisters, and I will reconvene on the anniversary of his death and not only celebrate his life, as our faith suggests, but also mark the time as the end of the mourning period. Not to forget him but to celebrate and honor him.

Caregivers' reactions to the loss of a parent or loved one is an intensely personal event. No two people grieve alike. Grief is hard work. There are tears, fears, and feelings of helplessness. And then, no tears are left. In the beginning you feel like you are in limbo. You think you cannot bear it any longer. And then, something new happens like a holiday, and you have to turn that corner. Guilt is a natural process of loss and grief. Unfortunately, if we focus on guilt for too long, we can slow down the healing process and waste valuable strength on useless thoughts.

Grief is a stressor of very high proportions. Even with advanced planning, end-of-life decisions are very taxing, and the caregiver may often delegate end-of-life tasks to others, not because she cannot do it, but because she is drained of emotions and energy. Because grief uses enormous quantities of energy, it may cause debilitating stress. The process is very draining, but one must recognize that there is no way to get over or around loss: it must be experienced. Every so often, you need to take a break from grieving, just like any other physical labor. Respite allows you to reenergize and replenish yourself. If you fail to do so, you will burn out.

When sudden death occurs, one often dies alone. An unexpected death may be a blessing for those who die, but for those left behind, the mourning process is more difficult and takes longer. There may be a feeling of a lack of closure. There may also be feelings of regret and anguish and a sense that you let them down. Because a loved one may have died alone, no matter how much effort, time, and love the caregiver provided, this can lead to deep feelings and guilt. As a caregiver, an attachment has been severed, and the feelings of guilt compound the loss.

SPOUSAL BEREAVEMENT

Oftentimes, the grief of a long-term spouse is one of the most heart-wrenching losses one can experience. Numbness, denial, and disorientation follow the terrible loneliness that can overwhelm at this time. When a bond is broken, widows and widowers report an unbearable feeling of isolation. They must grieve not only for the present loss, but also for loss of a way of life they have known for years and the special dreams they will no longer share with their spouse (e.g., retirement). One of the hardest decisions for widows is deciding to live again. Attending a support group, making new friends, and trying to move on are transformations that help with the core of this grief.

Statistics have shown that a spouse is especially vulnerable to experiencing his or her own death for up to two years after the partner's death. The widowed person cannot think she is wrong when she wants to get back into society. She may not consider something such as dating, but she can talk on the phone with friends. The spouse must be aware and open to the valuable and beautiful things that surround her and tap into the winning ways that give her nourishment.

The single most common loss for adults is the loss of a parent. It is consistent with the laws of nature. Although an "adult child," you are still the child of your parent. When a parent dies, many adult children feel orphaned. Feelings of rootlessness and loneliness can be an expected reaction. One woman expressed it eloquently when she said, "I always had my mother to call for some information or news of the family. She always was the pipeline for our whole family. Once my mother died, I felt like an orphan with no one special to turn to. My aunts and sisters were not enough."

Usually one has attachments outside of the parental relationship (e.g., to one's spouse, children, and friends). For some people, this can alleviate grief. Unfortunately, the opposite is sometimes true for others. No matter what age, feeling regressed and childish is a normal response to loss. The relationship we have with our parents is unlike any other. For better or for worse, all of us have parts of our parents as parts of ourselves. No one may ever love you so unconditionally as your parent. And maybe no one should.

Not all parent–child relationships are healthy and positive. When they are not, feelings are more complicated. In these situations, conflicts, anger, stress, and guilt are harder to resolve.

When a parent is dying, part of you is dying as well. The loss will resonate greatly. Many feelings arise after the immediate death. Your own mortality is staring at you in the mirror. A person may feel it most when something reminds them of their loved one, or when they hear something they wish they could share with that loved one.

When will grief be over? Grief is at odds with our age of instant messages, instant coffee, and instant satisfaction. It can reappear when you least expect it or be chronic and persistent if unexpressed. Some people can complete the process of grief in a month. For others, the process can take years. Grief, unfortunately, is not a process to be hurried. As the saying says, "time heals all wounds." The hurt may never completely go away, but the pain is usually lessened as time goes on.

Erich Lindemann (1944) termed the phrase "grief work" to describe the tasks and process that one must complete to resolve grief. In this grief work, not only the actual person you have lost is mourned, but also the hopes, dreams, wishes, fantasies, unfulfilled expectations, and feelings you had for that person. The widow, for example, must grieve not only for the present loss, but also for the special dreams that will not come (e.g., the retirement they will not share).This includes liberation from the loss and the ability to form new relationships.

Grief changes us. It shapes us, and oftentimes it is an opportunity for growth. The most difficult part is allowing the growth to take place in its on way—it cannot be directed. There are no defined marks of change—no sudden leaps. But slowly, very slowly, more energy is available. The world feels different when we grieve. When we change, we slowly begin to transcend our grief. Giving up is not an option. A few steps forward and often great steps back take us toward restored strength and energy. And through some miracle, we become more adventurous, more curious, better risk takers, more compassionate, grateful for every day, less fearful, and believing in ourselves and love. Life begins to get back to almost normal.

When I was 21 years old, I lost my firstborn. My physician advised my husband and me to "get pregnant immediately," and we would "forget." Death did not touch me again personally for many years, until my father died. It was then that every loss I had experienced in my life surfaced, and I experienced a profound sense of grief. I had never resolved the grief from losing my firstborn child. In a way, I believe it was a blessing in disguise. I had always repressed part of myself until I resolved my early grief and was able to move on during other losses.

One of my patients was still grieving for her mother who had passed away 40 years prior. Even though she was unconsciously repressing her grief, it resurfaced as depression in her later years. During the death of her husband, she resolved both instances of grief through counseling and hard work. This woman carried her grief around with her for years before coming to terms with it. By avoiding the work of resolving grief, some will carry their grief until they die. It may be impossible to avoid this for some people, but understanding that new attachment figures are available and reaching out to these figures will provide the nurturance needed.

SPECIFIC SUGGESTIONS FOR RESOLVING GRIEF

The following are strategies and reminders that have helped families ease the pain of grief:

1. *Stay physically present.* Live in the "now."
2. *You can keep your loved one's memory alive while still living your life.* Understand that in the death of a loved one, healthy grief does not mean abandoning a loved one but rather developing a relationship based on loving memories. Grief does not erase love.
3. *Do not second-guess your caretaking.* For example—Did I do enough for the care-receiver? Was I kind and considerate enough? Did I spend enough time with him or her? Did I help my family get through it? What's done is done.
4. *Be honest with yourself.* When you're feeling lousy, acknowledge the feeling without trying to gloss it over. Accept the feeling, do the grief work, and move on.
5. *Use affirmations.* Affirmations always start with "I." Ask yourself, how do I want to feel?
   - I'm doing the best I can.
   - I can handle it.
   - I am peaceful.
   - I will transcend this grief.

Write these affirmations on sticky notes and put them around your house.

6. *Make a conscious decision to get through the grief and the loss—care about yourself.* Give yourself hope for the future.
7. *Change your environment.* Spending all your time in one place may exacerbate your grief, especially if it is a place you shared with your loved one. Go for a walk, see a movie, or attend a religious service.
8. *Give yourself permission to feel your loss and to grieve.* Recognize and accept that all feelings are normal during grief.
9. *Recognize that you are unique, and this is your loss.* What others think does not make any difference. There is no correct way to grieve. The way is yours. Do not let others' needs determine your grieving experience. Do not let anyone minimize your loss.
10. *We can relieve the stress of grief in an appropriate way.* Walking, exercising, screaming, deep breathing, and so on are all appropriate expressions of grief. The experience of release is part of the healing process.

11. Keep reminding yourself that growth can come from grief.
12. Remember to reinvest in new friends or a support group.
13. Remember that no one can take the pain away.
14. *Remember that people often avoid bereaved persons.* There is an unintentional stigma attached to those in grief. People do not like to see others in grief—it reminds them that grief at some point is inevitable in all our lives.
15. *Grief can be especially potent during holidays.* Bring a picture of your loved one to the family gathering the first year.
16. *Acknowledge your feelings.* Otherwise the loss will not be resolved. For example—"I am feeling anger." Then find some way to express it.
17. *Mourners desperately need the support and assistance of others.* Do not isolate yourself—share the laughter and the crying. A sensitive person will never be immune to feelings of sadness from the death of a loved one, but it may help to experience the grief with others. This may mean going to a therapist, joining a support group, or discussing one's feelings with a good friend.
18. Little credence is given these days to those who mourn the loss of an aged individual. For instance, a 90-year-old parent may have lived a long and thorough life, but you will miss him nonetheless.
19. *Practice mindfulness.* Mindfulness is a conscious process. Focus your attention on what you are experiencing moment by moment. Bring full awareness to your experience.
20. There is life after grief.

Bereavement offers us the opportunity to find ourselves once again. When we suffer a major loss, we are caught within forces of transition, much like the ones we experienced in adolescence. Maturity comes when we accept responsibility and a new and different life—all transitions thereafter are similar. The real strength of helping someone experience a "good death" is that is beneficial for both parties. You not only help your loved one, but also provide a template for the next generation.

After the caretaking process is over, and one has been a witness to someone's life and death, the process of attachment behavior becomes evermore valuable, and Freud's question in *Totem and Taboo* (1912)—"How can we attribute to the psychological continuity in the sequence of generations, and what are the ways and means employed by one generation in order to hand on its mental status to the next one?"—is relevant. We will wonder about how we ourselves will experience death, and by thinking about these matters, we will conquer the fear of aging and dying.

Eventually we will all travel the road into old age, illness, and death. Caregivers and care-receivers alike, we all have choices regarding how we approach living through the longevity revolution. If the experience is considered burdensome and fearful, those generations that follow will think of the past as "unreal." William James penetrates the heart of the matter when he says that the worlds of previous generations, whose objects are neither interesting nor important, we treat simply negatively, and we brand them unreal. James asks the question, "Do humans have the ability to see the relationships that sustain them?" (1980).

13

Conclusion

Being educated about caregiving and knowing that one can prepare for its possibility creates a kind of respect for what it truly is. This is a stage in life that most of us will face someday. When respect is high, people will accept that planning for a new stage is part of a celebration of life. Often unacknowledged and unexpressed fears only keep us from a recognition of what we may some-day become. Denial of our own aging, for some, only induces fear. One cannot be on top of everything all the time because when in the midst of caregiving for an older person, emotional obstacles cause confusing and challenging issues. The relationship between the caregiver and care-receiver brings us face to face with the reflections of ourselves and provides a greater reflection of society.

To realize these potential rewards, the caregiver and the care-receiver have to be honest with on another and cognizant of the demands being placed on them. Such honesty can help relieve stress, loneliness, burnout, and despair in caretaking. Caretaking can be an opportunity for the caregiver to affirm that a rich receding past joins us, and this affirmation can unlock one's own potential for growth and happiness.

Sustenance and Hope for Caregivers of Elderly Parents searches for a new paradigm that will help families who were formerly unprepared for the dependency needs of an ill parent. Being prepared, for the caretaker, means changing the conversation between generations and having self-respect and confidence that caregiving can lead to a spiritual awakening of oneself.

Thinking about these matters means surveying certain distinctive prop-erties of adulthood and taking a look at the ominous significance of these properties such as the problems people encounter in caregiving, sustaining life, and the fear of negative consequences in thinking about the future. This is more dangerous ground than remaining innocent and helpless.

In his 1912 book *Totem and Taboo,* Freud asked two questions that might be relevant to society today and future generations: "How much can we attribute to the psychological continuity in the sequence of generations, and what are the ways and means employed by one generation in order to hand on its mental status to the next one?" (13). One of the ways is through the art of caregiving.

Appendices

Appendix A: 60 Proven Practices for Stress Reduction

1. Do not strive for perfection. No one will complain if you take some time for yourself and let the dishes wait.
2. Prepare for the next day the night before. Make lunches, set out clothes, etc.
3. Find ways of making everyday experiences fulfilling.
4. Get some fresh air every day. If it is cold, and you cannot go out, open the door and breathe in oxygen and breathe out stressful thinking.
5. Get up a half-hour earlier in the morning. Most glitches can start in the morning.
6. A half-hour of exercise every day does more than three hours on the weekend.
7. Find something at work that is pleasurable. Look at the person serving you in the cafeteria or at the coffee shop with gratitude.
8. Even if you have a good memory, write things down in an appointment book.
9. Make double copies of all keys, and carry your parent's keys on your key ring. Find a place outdoors to hide a key.
10. Do today what you want to do today. Procrastination only creates more stress.
11. Plan ahead and ask for help if you need it. Most people are happy to be asked to help out with caregiving.
12. Throw out or fix everything that does not work right. If your clock or can opener does not work, it is a constant aggravation.
13. Always have a second plan in your mind "just in case" of delays, losing your you loved one in the market, etc. (A cell phone is the best finder.)
14. Carry cell phones. When you cannot find your cell, have someone call your number.
15. Allow extra time for everything. People who are ill need more time for walking and getting on elevators.
16. Relaxing some standards will not end your life.

17. When things go wrong, try to think of at least one thing that went right.
18. Do not wait until your loved one calls saying he has no milk. Stock an emergency shelf of things you know he will need.
19. Count your own blessings, even the tiniest ones.
20. Practice prevention. Keep the gas filled, and try to keep things up to date. Things happen quickly.
21. Always take something to do and be prepared to wait. Reading in a doctor's office can take the edge off waiting for reports.
22. Carry a list of all medications, emergency telephone numbers, pacemaker information, glasses, and hearing aid numbers.
23. Ask lots of question and take a few minutes to repeat the answers back. If you listen and take notes, it saves hours of callbacks.
24. Take quiet time for yourself every day. Say no to extra projects. Remember that everyone always asks the busiest person for favors. That is why they are always busy.
25. Take a long bath, have a manicure or a facial, or get your hair done.
26. Remember the old Basque saying: "Show up—Pay attention—Tell the truth without blame or judgment, and do not be attached to the outcome."
27. Do nothing you have to lie about later.
28. Simplify everything, and if you want to modify things later, you can.
29. Stay away from chronic worriers or complainers. Make new friends who are non-worriers.
30. Count to 100 or 1,000 before you say something that could make things worse.
31. Wear earplugs if your home is too noisy.
32. Sleep restores your energy, so get enough sleep.
33. Keep a journal. It will help you clarify your own thoughts.
34. Remember that negative thoughts cause negative action.
35. Talk out concerns or problems with a friend. If something is bugging you, turn it around.
36. Be as organized as you can. Have a place near the door for your cell phone, keys, and everyday necessities. Misplacing things is very stressful and finding them time-consuming.
37. Do one thing at a time. If two people are talking to you, tell one to wait.
38. Monitor your own body for stress signals. If your breathing is heavy, or your muscles are knotted, take some deep breaths.
39. If something is making your fearful, try to visualize it. Take time to go over every step or part of an event and imagine how well you will do.
40. When deadlines get in the way of finishing a project, use some diversion. Take your mind off the task, and when you return, you will be more focused.
41. Avoid things that wind you up. Do not spend time with people who bore you.
42. Learn that one day at a time is a good mantra.
43. Every single day, be kind to yourself and do something you truly love.
44. Do someone a favor.
45. Look your best. It just makes you feel good.
46. Schedule a day away from all illness or caretaking.
47. Do positive self-talk: I love myself, I love my brainpower, and I love being my age.

48. Weekends are for changing pace, thinking, and planning. Book a room in a hotel.
49. Do the tasks you dislike first or learn to delegate them to someone else. A cleaning woman may love doing your grocery shopping or spending an extra hour on something you always do but hate doing.
50. Remember that we live in a pretty imperfect world, so forgive people and events. All of us do the best we can.
51. Do not be a risk taker while caretaking. Having a lot on your mind just causes confusion.
52. Do one thing at a time. Stay focused on that one thing. If you think about all the other things going on or what you have to do, your focus for what is important gets lost.
53. Change your surroundings. You will see things from a different angle.
54. Take one step at a time. And say to yourself, "I will take one step at a time with this."
55. If someone is lying to you, go right to the source immediately. Do not dwell on it. Find the truth.
56. Once in a while, you have to give in and say you made a mistake.
57. Raise your toes every night.
58. Criticism only causes more stress for everyone. Think before you criticize.
59. Do an act of kindness.
60. Have a good belly laugh every day. Look for people who make you laugh.
61. Stress is energy. Anything you do to let go off stress recharges your own energy.
62. First things first. And that means you. Take care of yourself first.

APPENDIX B: MINDFULNESS

Have you ever lost your keys and found them in your pocket but then could not remember why you put them there instead of your usual place? Have you gone to the second floor of your home and then could not remember why you went there? Have you ever filled out a form and forgotten a very important detail? These are examples of mindlessness. You have so many things on your mind at one time, and you lose focus. The mindless state is the opposite of meditation, where we train the mind to pay attention to a single focus. When our single focus is on experiencing the moment, being fully present in any activity we are performing, we are practicing mindfulness, a kind of a meditation in daily life. The more mindful you are, the more efficiently, comfortably, and skillfully you can walk through life. So another way of thinking about mindfulness is tuning into the fullest experience that life has to offer.

Mindfulness is the practice of learning to pay attention to what is occurring within our field of experience from moment to moment. It is particularly useful for people learning to elicit the relaxation response because it allows them to extend the benefits of relaxation in more areas of their daily lives. This practice involves a combination of slowing down, doing one activity at a time, and bringing full awareness to both outer activity and inner experience. It provides a potentially powerful antidote to the common causes of stress—such as time-pressure, distraction, agitation, and worry.

Mindfulness can be directed toward sensations in the body, heightening awareness and inviting relaxation. We can also be mindful toward our emotions, exploring their impact on the body. We can be mindful toward our own thinking process: we become aware of how afflicting thoughts affect our bodies and gradually retrain our minds, which will directly improve our heath.

The practice of mindfulness is to maintain full awareness from moment to moment.

The breath is the focus that integrates and connects each activity.

Mindfulness is waking up to the present reality, doing one activity (or Non-activity) at a time with total attention.

By training the mind and body to focus at the beginning of each new Activity, sustained concentration begins to develop and we have a Tool that keeps jogging the mind's tendency to become dull and distracted.

Inspired by gentle intentionality, we celebrate in small ways the passage Through the day, honoring each activity with mindful attention.

References

Goldstein, Joseph. *The Experience of Insight: A Simple Guide to Buddhist Meditation.* Boston: Shambhala, 1983.

Thich Naht. *The Miracle of Mindfulness: A Manual on Meditation.* Boston: Beacon Press, 1976.

Appendix C: Mini Relaxation Exercises

These exercises can be done with your eyes open or with them closed in a safe place. These exercises can be done anywhere and anytime. No one will know you are doing them. Do not close eyes while driving.

They should start with taking a deep breath and repeating to yourself, "I am at peace." Switch over to diaphragmatic breathing; if you are having trouble, try breathing in through your nose and out through your mouth, or take a deep breath. You should feel your stomach rising about an inch as you breathe in, and falling about an inch as you breathe out. If this is difficult for you, lie on your back or on your stomach; you will be more aware of your breathing pattern. Remember, it is impossible to breathe diaphragmatically if you are holding your stomach in.

Mini Version 1

Count very slowly to yourself from 10 down to zero. One number for each breath. Thus, with the first diaphragmatic breath, you say "10" to yourself, with the next breath, you say "9," and so on. If you start feeling light-headed or dizzy, slow down the counting. When you get to "zero," see how you are feeling. If you are feeling better, great! If not, try doing it again.

Mini Version 2

As you inhale, count very slowly up to four; as you exhale, count slowly back down to one. Thus, as you inhale, you say to yourself, "one, two, three, four"; as you exhale, you say to yourself "four, three, two, one." Do this several times.

Mini Version 3

After each inhalation, pause for a few seconds; after you exhale, pause again for a few seconds. Do this for several breaths.

Good Times to Do a Mini

When put on hold during a phone call, while waiting in a doctor's office, when someone says something that bothers you, when waiting for a phone call, while in the dentist's chair, when you feel overwhelmed by what you need to accomplish in the near future, while standing in line anywhere.

APPENDIX D: THOUGHTS THAT CAUSE STRESS

I must be perfect at all times.
I must love my parents no matter what they say or do.
I must keep the truth from them and tell no one else.
I must always be competent.
Making a mistake is a terrible thing.
There is a perfect solution for every problem.
I must not cry or show my true feelings.
Everything is in my control.
I do not need any help.
Strong people do not ask for help.
I cannot take any criticism. I am always right.
I cannot change the way I think.
Everyone who loves me should do exactly as I say.
Everyone should see things my way.
No one else knows better than I.
There is no way I can take any time for myself.
Stress is a killer. (In fact, stress can be an opportunity for growth and change.)

APPENDIX E: RESOURCES FOR CAREGIVERS

General Services

Agecare
999 Vanderbilt Beach Road

Suite 607
Naples, Florida 34108
Web site: http://www.Agingcare.com
886-627-2467

Today's Caregiver
3005 Green Street
Hollywood, Florida 33020
Web site: http://www.Caregiver.com
1-800-829-2734
Distributes *Caregiver* magazine and online edition

Rosalynn Carter Institute for Caregiving
800 GSW Drive
Georgia Southwestern State University
Americus, Georgia 31709-4379
229-928-1234
e-mail: rci@canes.gsw.edu
Web site: http://www.rosalynncarter.org

Well Spouse Association
63 West Main Street, Suite H
Freehold, NBJ 07728
800-838-0879
e-mail: info@wellspouse.org
Web site: http://www.wellspouse.org

The Leeza Gibbons Memory Foundation
888-655-3392
Go to a caring space at http://www.leezasplace.org
Senior Site
Web site: Seniors-site.com

For Adults 50+ or Their Children and Caregivers

International Center for Disability Resources on the Internet
Main Office
5212 Covington Bend Drive
Raleigh, NC 27613
919-349-6661
icdri@icdri.org
Web site: http://www.icdri.org/

Lotsa Helping Hands
http://www.lotsahelpinghands.com

The National Alliance for Caregiving
4720 Montgomery Lane, 5th floor
Bethesda, Maryland 20815
301-718-8444
e-mail: info@caregiving.org
Web site: http://www.caregiving.org

National Family Caregivers Association
10400 Connecticut Avenue
Suite 500
Kensington, Maryland 20895-3944
800-896-3650
e-mail: Info@thefamilycaregiver.org
Web site: http://www.nfcacares.org/

9 Ways to Make It Easier for the Caregiver

1. *Compromise.* Work hard to avoid family fights and resentments if you are a sibling or a relative of the primary caregiver. Do not let old issues pull you apart. This is the time to stick together.
2. *Coordinate.* Offer your services if you have skill with insurance forms, Medicare, or legal documents. Try to help prepare a game plan for when an illness becomes more severe or fatal. Adult kids often avoid that conversation.
3. *Encourage.* Help the caregiver find some type of professional support. If he or she is not comfortable with in-person support groups, suggest online chat rooms. Many organizations have them.
4. *Facilitate.* Ask somebody who can be objective—a cleric, a social worker—to act as a negotiator in stressful situations where the caregiver may be struggling with the patient, other family members, or even health care providers.
5. *Investigate.* Find books, go to Web sites, or get in touch with organizations that can help caregivers learn about the illness of the person for whom they are caring; it will save them time.
6. *Organize.* Work with the caregiver to make a list of people who can be called upon for different duties, if needed. If time is what is needed, help the caregiver schedule friends to work shifts.
7. *Discuss.* Ask the caregiver to tell his or her story or keep a journal. Writing things down can be a release and might help others better understand the caregiver's needs.
8. *Plan.* Tell the caregiver about the services you can offer, and be specific. Making yourself clear makes it easier for the caregiver to ask for your help.
9. *Socialize.* Create events for the caregiver and, if possible, the person for whom he or she is caring. Include them in community and family activities.

BIBLIOGRAPHY

Abramson, L., Seligman, M. E., & Teasdale, J. "Learned helplessness in humans: Critique and reformulation." *Journal of Abnormal Psychology,* 87 (1980): 49–74.

Alighieri, Dante. *The Devine Comedy.* New York: Bantam Books. 1982.

Balint, M. *The Basic Fault.* London: Tavistock Clinic. 1968.

Balint, M. *Primary Love and Psychoanalytic Technique.* New York: Liveright. 1965.

Barsamian, Gloria. "Care arrangements for an aging parent: The reaction of adult children." Master's thesis, Harvard University. 1985.

Barsamian, Gloria, & Kelly, M. E. *Pilot Study to Analyze How Elderly Patients' Levels of Self-Efficacy Determine Their Behavior Upon Discharge and Subsequent Return Home from a Hospital. And How Adult Children and Grandchildren of These Elderly Parents, Perceive the Efficacy of Their Parents or Grandparents.* Burlington, MA: Lahey Clinic Medical Center. 1988.

Bateson, Gregory. *Mind and Nature.* New York: Bantam Books. 1978.

Bateson, Gregory. *Steps to an Ecology of Mind.* New York: Ballantine Books. 1972.

Beck, Aaron, T. *Love Is Never Enough.* New York: Harper and Row Publishers. 1988.

Beck, A. T., Kovacs, M., & Weissman, A. "Hopelessness and suicidal behavior." *Journal of the American Medical Association* 234, no. 11 (December 15, 1975): 1146–1149.

Beck, A. T., Lester, D., Trexler, L., & Weissman, A. "The measurement of the hopelessness scale. *Journal of Consulting and Clinical Psychology* 42, no. 6 (1974): 861–865.

Benson, Herbert. *The Relaxation Response.* New York: William Morrow. 1976.

Benson, Herbert, & Stuart, Eileen M. *The Wellness Book.* New York: Birch Lane Press. 1992.

Blenker, M. "Generational relations." In *Social Structure & the Family,* ed. E. Shanas & G. Strieb. Boston: Harvard University Press. 1962.

Bok, Sissela. *Lying: Moral Choice in Public and Private Life.* New York: Panthoen. 1979.

Bowlby, J. *Attachment and Loss: Attachment.* (Vol. 1). New York: Basic. 1969.

Bowlby, J. "Attachment and loss: Retrospect and prospect." *American Journal of Orthopsychiatry* 52 (1982): 664–78.

Bowlby, J. *Attachment and Loss: Separation, Anxiety and Anger.* (Vol. 2). New York: Basic. 1973.

Bowlby, J., & Melges, F. "Types of hopelessness in the psychopathological process." *Archives of General Psychiatry* 20 (1969): 689–99.

Brody, Jane E. "World enough and time for 'a good death.'" *New York Times*. October 31, 2006.

Brody, S., Poulshock, S., & Masciocci, C. "The family care unit: A major consideration in the long term support system." *Gerontologist* 18 (1978): 556–61.

Buber, Martin. *I and Thou*. New York: Macmillan Publishing Company. 1958.

Butler, R. N. *The Benefits and Challenges of Living a Long Life: The Longevity Revolution*. New York: PublicAffairs. 2008.

Butler, R. N. "Life review: An interpretation of reminiscence in the aged." *Psychiatry* 26 (1963): 65–76.

Butler, R. N. "Why survive?" *Being Old in America*. New York: Harper & Row. 1975.

Butsch, R. "Reviewing the reviews: A note on the portrayal of the elderly in films and reviews." *Gerontologist* (1980): 496–502.

Cahill, Susan. *Mothers*. New York: Penguin. 1988.

Carp, F., & Carp, A. "Mental health characteristics and acceptance-rejection of old age." *American Journal of Orthopsychiatry* 51, no. 2 (1981): 230–41.

Casey, Nell. *An Uncertain Inheritance*. New York: HarperCollins. 2007.

Cousins, Norman. *Head First (The Biology of Hope)*. New York: E. P. Dutton. 1989.

Cousins, Norman. *Anatomy of an Illness*. New York: Bantam. 1978.

Cousins, Norman. "An interview with Norman Cousins." *The Coordinator* (April 1983).

D'Alessandro, Frank. *Sacco and Vanzetti*. New York: Jay Street Publishers. 1997.

Davis, J., Hall, S. S. & Usita, P. M. "Role ambiguity in family caregiving." *Journal of Applied Gerontology* (1982): 20–39.

Dengler, Eartha, Khalife, Katherine, & Skulski, Ken. *Lawrence Massachusetts*. Dover, NH: Arcadia. 1995.

Dyck, Arthur, J. *On Human Care*. New York: Partheon Press. 1977.

Erikson, Erik H. *Adulthood*. New York: Norton. 1978.

Erikson, Erik H. *Childhood and Society*. New York: Norton. 1950.

Erikson, E., & Erikson, J. "On generativity and identity: From a conversation with J. & E. Erikson." *Harvard Educational Review*, 51, no. 2 (1981).

Fairborn, W. R. *An Object-Relations Theory of the Personality*. New York: Basic. 1954.

Fairborn, W. R. *Psychoanalytic Studies of the Personality*. London: Tavistock. 1952.

Farkas, Susan W. "Impact of chronic illness on the patient's spouse." *Health and Social Work* (1980): 3946.

Fingerman, Karen L. *Aging Mothers and Their Adult Daughters*. New York: Springer. 2001.

Frank, Arthur. *At the Will of the Body*. New York. Houghton Mifflin. 1991.

Frankl, Viktor. E. *Man's Search for Meaning*. New York: Simon and Schuster. 1959.

Freud, S. *Beyond the Pleasure Principle*. Standard edition of the complete works. London: Hogarth. 1920.

Freud, S. *Totem and Taboo*. Trans. James Strachey. London: Hogarth. 1912.

Fried, M. "Grieving for a lost home." In *Stress and Coping*, ed. A. Monat & R. Lazarus, 375–88. New York: Columbia University Press. 1977.

Friedan, Betty. *The Fountain of Age*. New York: Simon and Schuster. 1993.

Fulton, R., Gottesman, D., & Owen, G. "Loss, social change and the prospect of mourning." *Death Education* 6 (1982): 137–53.

Gallo, Patrick J. *Old Bread New Wine: A Portrait of the Italian-Americans*. Chicago: Nelson-Hall. 1981.

Gambino, Richard. *Blood of My Blood*. Garden City, NY: Doubleday. 1974.

Garber, J., & Seligman, M. (eds.). *Human Helplessness: An Attributional Analysis*. New York: Academic. 1980.

Getzel, G. "Social work with family caregivers to the aged." *Social Casework* 62 (1981): 201–9.

Gibson, M. J., & Houser, A. "Valuing the invaluable: A new look at the economic value of family caregiving." *AARP Public Policy Institute* 10 (2007).

Gillick, Muriel R. *The Denial of Aging.* Cambridge, MA: Harvard University Press. 2006.

Goldhor Lerner, Harriet. *The Dance of Anger.* New York: Harper & Row. 1985.

Goldhor Lerner, Harriet. *The Dance of Deception.* New York: HarperCollins. 1993.

Goldhor Lerner, Harriet. *The Dance of Intimacy.* New York: Harper & Row. 1989.

Graboys, Thomas & Zhuetlin, Peter. *Life in the Balance.* New York: Union Square Press. 2008.

Greene, Kelly. "Solving the caregiving puzzle." *Wall Street Journal* (November 15, 2008), R1–10.

Gross, Jane. "For the elderly, being heard about life's end." *New York Times.* May 5, 2008.

Hartford, M., & Parsons, R. "Groups with relatives of dependent older adults." *Gerontologist* 22 no. 3 (1982): 394–98.

He, Wan, Sengupta, Velkoff, & Desarros. *65+ in the United States: 2005.* U.S. Department of Health and Human Services. National Institute of Health. National Institute of Aging. U.S. Census Bureau. U.S. Department of Commerce. 2005.

Holmes, T. H., & Rahe, R. H. "The social readjustment scale." *Psychosomatic Medicine* 11 (1967): 213–18.

Horney, Karen. *Feminine Psychology.* New York: Norton. 1967.

Horney, Karen. *Neurosis and Human Growth.* New York: Norton. 1950.

Horney, Karen. *Our Inner Conflicts.* New York: Norton. 1966.

Hunter-Cooper, Joan, et al. *Fourteen Friends' Guide to Elder-Caring.* New York: Broadway Books. 1999.

Isay, Jane. *Walking on Eggshells: Navigating the Delicate Relationship between Adult Children and Parents.* New York: Doubleday. 2007.

Jacobs, Barry. *The Emotional Survival Guide for Caregivers.* New York: Guilford Press. 2006.

James, W. *The Principles of Psychology.* (Vol. 2). New York: Dover. 1980.

Janis, Irving L. *Stress and Frustration.* New York: Harcourt Brace Jovanich. 1971.

Johnson, D. G. "Abuse of the elderly." *Nurse Practitioner* (January 1981): 29–32.

Kabat-Zinn, Jon. *Full Catastrophe Living.* New York: Doubleday. 1990.

Kabat-Zinn, Jon. *Wherever You Go—There You Are.* New York: Hyperion. 1994.

Kahana, R. J. "The aging survivor of the holocaust. Discussion and reconciliation between generations, a last chance." *Journal of Geriatric Psychiatry* 14, no. 2 (1981): 225–35.

Kane, R., & Kane, R. "Alternatives to institutional care of the elderly." *Gerontologist* 20 (1980): 249–59.

Kane, R., & Kane, R. "Long term care in six countries: implications for the U.S.D.H.E.W." Publ #NH 761207, USGPO, Washington, D.C. 1976.

Kane, Robert L., & Joan C. West. *It Shouldn't Be This Way.* Nashville: Vanderbilt University Press. 2005.

Kegan, Robert. *The Evolving Self.* Cambridge, MA: Harvard University Press. 1982.

Kleinman, Arthur. *The Illness Narratives.* New York: Basic Books. 1988.

Kleinman, Arthur. *What Really Matters.* New York: Oxford University Press. 2006.

Kohn, M., Donley, C., & Wear, D. *Literature and Aging.* Kent, OH: The Kent University Press. 1992.

Kobasa, S. "Stressful life events, personality and health: An inquiry into hardiness." *Journal of Personality and Social Psychology* 37 (1979): 1–11.

Koch, Tom. *Age Speaks for Itself: Silent Voices of the Elderly.* Westport, CT: Praeger. 2000.

Kuba, Cheryl. *Navigating the Journey of Aging Parents: What Care Receivers Want.* New York: Routledge. 2006.

Kübler-Ross, Elisabeth. *Death: The Final Stage of Growth.* Upper Saddle River, NJ: Prentice-Hall. 1975.

Laing, R. D. *The Politics of the Family.* New York: Vintage Books. 1972.

Langer, E. J. "Old age: An artifact?" In *Aging Biology and Behavior.* St. Louis, MO: Academic Press. 1981.

Langer, E. J. *The Psychology of Control.* Beverly Hills: Sage. 1983.

Langer, Ellen. *Mindfulness.* Reading, MA: Addison Wesley. 1989.

Langer, Ellen. *The Power of Mindful Learning.* Reading, MA: Addison Wesley. 1997.

Lazarus, Richard S., & Monat, Alan. *Stress and Coping.* New York: Columbia University Press. 1977.

Legge, James, *The Chinese Classics,* Five volumes, Hong Kong: Hong Kong University Press. 1960.

Lidz, T. *The Person.* New York: Basic. 1965.

Lieberman, G. L. "Children of the elderly as natural helpers: Some demographic considerations." *American Journal of Community Psychology* 6, no. 5 (1978): 489–98.

Li Fu Chen. *The Confucian Way.* London: KPI Ltd. 1987.

Lindeman, E. "Symptomatology and management of acute grief." *American Journal of Psychiatry* 101 (1944): 141–8.

Marchinoe, William P. *Italian Americans of Greater Boston.* Charleston, SSC: Arcadia. 1999.

Marris, P. "Attachment and society." In *The Place of Attachment in Human Behavior,* ed. J. Hinde. & C. Murray. New York: Basic. 1982.

McGoldrick, M., Pearce, J. K., & Giordano, J. (eds.). *Ethnicity and Family Therapy.* New York: Guilford Press. 1982.

McGraw, L. A., & Walker A. "Negotiating care: Ties between aging mothers and their caregiving daughters." *Journal of Gerontology; Social Sciences* 59B no. 6 (2004): 324–32.

Melges, F. T., & Bowlby, J. "Types of hopelessness in psychopathological process." *Archives of General Psychiatry* 20 (1969): 690–99.

Menninger, K. "Regulatory devices of the ego under major stress." In *Stress and Coping,* ed. A. Monat & R. Lazarus, 159–73. New York: Columbia. 1977.

MetLife Juggling Act Study*, Balancing Caregiving with Work and the Costs of Caregiving,* Met Life Mature Market Institute. November 1999.

Morris, Virginia. *How to Care for Aging Parents.* New York: Workman. 1996.

Moskowitz, Faye. *Her Face in the Mirror.* Boston: Beacon Press. 1994.

National Association of Caregiving and American Association of Retired Persons. *Caregiving in the U.S.* 2004.

National Family Caregivers Association (NFCA), *Caregiving Statistics Survey of Self-Identified Family Caregivers.* 2001.

National Institute on Aging (NIA), *Dramatic Changes in U.S. Aging Highlighted in New Census: Impact of Baby Boomers Anticipated.* National Institute of Aging; Census Bureau. March 9, 2006.

National Institute on Aging (NIA), *Dramatic Changes in U.S.* Census Bureau; National Institute of Aging, press release. March 9, 2008.

Neugarten, B. L. "Time, age and the life cycle." *American Journal of Psychiatry* 136, no. 7 (1979): 887–94.

Neugarten, B., & Guttman, D. "Age sex roles and personality in middle age: A thematic apperception study." *Psychological Monograph* 72, no. 17 (1958).

Oakes, W., & Curtis, N. "Learned helplessness: Not dependent upon cognitions, attributions or other phenomenal experiences." *Journal of Personality,* 50, no. 4 (1982): 387–408.

Olsen, Tillie. *Tell Me a Riddle.* New York: Dell. 1961.

O'Neil, M., & Reiss, S. "Adult's perception of their mother: A life-span analysis." *The Psychological Record,* 34 (1984): 333–42.

Osgood, Nancy and Sontz. *The Science and Practice of Gerontology.* Westport, CT: Greenwood Press. 1989.

Owen, G., Fulton, R., & Markunsen, E. "Death at a distance: A study of family survivors." *Omega* 13, no. 3 (1982): 191–225.

Puleo, Stephen. *The Boston Italians.* Boston: Beacon Press. 2007.

Raia, P. A. "Helping patients and families to take control." *Psychiatric Annals* 24, no. 4 (April 1994).

Ratna, L., & Davis, J. "Crisis intervention in psychogeriatrics." *British Journal of Psychiatry* 141 (1982): 296–301.

Ratna, L., & Davis, J. "Family therapy with the elderly mentally ill." *British Journal of Psychiatry* 145 (1984): 311–15.

Rinpoche, Sogyal. *The Tibetan Book of Living and Dying.* San Francisco: HarperCollins. 2003.

Rodin, J., & Langer, E. "Long term effects of a control-relevant intervention with the institutionalized aged." *Journal of Personality and Social Psychology* 35 (1977): 897–902.

Rollan, John. "The impact of illness on the family." In T*extbook of Family Practice.* ed. R. E. Rake. Philadelphia: W. B Saunders. 1990.

Rosenmayr, L. "Changes in relation of the multigenerational family" (An English summary of La Famille multigenerationale). Paper presented at the World Conference of the Institute de la vie, Vichy, France. 1977.

Roth, Philip. *Patrimony.* New York: Simon & Schuster. 1991.

Rubin, Lillian. *Tangled Lives.* Boston: Beacon Press. 2000.

Sacks, Oliver. *An Anthropologist on Mars.* New York: Alfred A. Knopf. 1995.

Sacks, Oliver. *The Man Who Mistook His Wife for a Hat.* New York: Simon & Schuster. 1985.

Schachter-Shalomi, Zalman. *From Age-ing to Sage-ing.* New York: Warner Books. 1995.

Schinto, Jeanne. *Huddle Fever.* New York: Alfred Knopf. 1995.

Schmidt, M. G. "Failing parent, aging children." *Journal of Gerontological Social Work* 2, no. 3 (1980).

Seelbach, W. "Correlates of aged parents filial responsibility expectations and realizations." *Family Coordinator* 27, no. 4 (1978): 341–50.

Seligman, M. *Helplessness: On Depression Development and Death.* San Francisco: Freeman. 1975.

Selye, H. *The Stress of Life.* New York; McGraw-Hill. 1965.

Shanas, E. "Family responsibility and the health of older people." *Journal of Gerontology,* 15 (1960): 408–11.

Shanas, E. *The Health of Older People.* Oxford: Cambridge University Press. 1962.

Shanas, E. "Social research on aging and the aged: where are we now?" *Mt. Sinai Journal of Medicine* 2 (1981): 283–91.

Shanas, E., & Streib, G. *Social Structure and the Family.* Englewood Cliffs, NJ: Prentice. 1965.

Shawler, Cleleste. "Empowerment of aging mothers and daughters in transition during a health crisis." *Qualitative Health Research* 17, no. 6 (2007).

Silver, R., Klos, D., & Wortman, C. "Cognitive affect, and behavior following uncontrollable outcomes: A response to current human helplessness research." *Journal of Personality* 50, no. 4 (1982): 480–514.

Silverstone, B. "Issues of the middle generation: responsibility, adjustment and growth." In *Aging Parents,* ed. P. Ragen. Los Angeles, CA: Andrus. 1979.

Simos, B. "Relations of adult children with aging parents." *Gerontologist* (1970): 135–39.

Skulski, Ken. *Lawrence Massachusetts* (Vol. II). Dover, NH: Arcadia. 1997.

Sohngen, M. "The experience of old age as depicted in contemporary novels: A supplementary bibliography. *Gerontologist* 303, no. 3 (June 21, 1981).

Somers, A. R. "Long term care for the elderly disabled." *New England Journal of Medicine* (July, 1982): 221–26.

Stein, Michael. *The Lonely Patient.* New York: HarperCollins. 2007.

Steinberg Turiel, Judith. *Our Parents, Ourselves.* Berkeley and Los Angeles: University of California Press. 2005.

Tannen, Deborah. *You're Wearing That?* New York: Random House. 2006.

Tennstedt, Sharon. *Family Caregiving in an Aging Society. Administration on Aging.* Presented at U.S. Administration on Aging Symposium; Longevity in the New American Century, Baltimore, MD, March 29, 1999.

Tolstoy, Leo. *The Death of Ivan Ilyich.* London: Penguin Books. 1960.

Townsend, P. "Health and incapacity in later life." In *Old People in Three Industrial Societies,* ed. E. Shanas et al. New York: Atherton. 1968.

Tuzil, T. "The agency role in helping children and their aging parents." *Social Casework* (May, 1978): 302–5.

Wansbrough, Henry. *The New Jerusalem Bible.* New York: Doubleday. 1985.

Watson, Burton. *The Analects of Confucius.* New York: Columbia University Press. 2007.

Watson, Bruce. *Bread and Roses.* New York: Viking Penguin. 2005.

Watson, Bruce. *Sacco and Vanzetti.* New York: Viking Penguin. 2007.

Weeks, J. R. "The role of family members in helping networks of older people." *Gerontologist* 4 (1981): 288–94.

Weiss, R. S. "Attachment in adult life." In *The Place of Attachment in Human Behavior,* ed. J. Hinde & C. Murray. New York: Basic. 1982.

Weiss, R. S. *Loneliness: The Experience of Social Isolation.* Cambridge, MA: MIT Press. 1974.

White, R. W. "Motivation reconsidered: The concept of competence." *Psychological Review* 66 (1959): 297–333.

Williams, T., Franklin, Hill, J., Faribank, M., & Knox, K. "Appropriate placement of the chronically ill and aged." *Journal of the American Medical Association* 11 (1973): 226.

Zarit, S. H. "Relatives of the impaired elderly; Correlates of feelings of burden. *Gerontologist* 6 (December 20, 1980): 649–55.

INDEX

About the Author

GLORIA G. BARSAMIAN graduated from Boston University and Harvard College. She completed postgraduate work at the Massachusetts School of Professional Psychology and Boston Family Institute. For 28 years at the Lahey Clinic Medical Center, her primary interest and research was intergenerational issues among adult children and elderly parents.

About the Series Editor

JULIE SILVER, MD, is an assistant professor, Harvard Medical School, Department of Physical Medicine and Rehabilitation, and is on the medical staff at Brigham & Women's, Massachusetts General, and Spaulding Rehabilitation hospitals in Boston, Massachusetts. Dr. Silver has authored, edited, or co-edited more than a dozen books, including medical textbooks and consumer health guides. She is also the chief editor of books at Harvard Health Publications. Dr. Silver has won many awards, including the American Medical Writers Association Solimene Award for Excellence in Medical Writing and the prestigious Lane Adams Quality of Life Award from the American Cancer Society. Silver is active in teaching health care providers how to write and publish, and she is the founder and director of an annual seminar facilitated by the Harvard Medical School Department of Continuing Education, "Publishing Books, Memoirs and Other Creative Non-Fiction."